FROM THE EDITORS OF
BIRDS & BLOOMS MAGAZINE

Gardening for Birds, Butterflies & Bees

FROM THE EDITORS OF
BIRDS & BLOOMS MAGAZINE

Gardening for Birds, Butterflies & Bees

*Everything you need to know to create
a wildlife habitat in your backyard.*

Gardening for Birds, Butterflies & Bees

©2018 RDA Enthusiast Brands, LLC

1610 N. 2nd Street, Suite 102,
Milwaukee, WI 53212-3906

International Standard Book Number:
978-1-61765-794-8 (Hardcover)
978-1-62145-303-1 (Paperback)
Library of Congress Control Number:
2018935175
Component Number: 118500047H

Front cover: Rolf Nussbaumer,
hummingbird; Richard Day/Daybreak
Imagery, butterfly; Richard Day/
Daybreak Imagery, oriole; Ikordela/
Shutterstock.com, bee

Back cover: Chas/Shutterstock.com,
cardinal; ray herrick/racinphoto.com,
butterfly; Heidi Hess, birdhouse; Brenda
Foubert, nuthatch

Photo credits on page 248 are hereby
made part of this copyright.

Printed in China
1 3 5 7 9 10 8 6 4 2   (Hardcover)
5 7 9 10 8 6 4   (Paperback)

contents

Baltimore oriole
at crabapple tree

INTRODUCTION

Birds, butterflies and bees rely on plants, trees and shrubs to survive and thrive.

That's why doing your part for the environment by establishing wildlife-friendly areas in your own backyard is so crucial. Chances are, your garden is already a welcoming space for all kinds of nature, but with a little extra research and planning, you can take your gardening a couple steps further and transform your yard into a healthier and happier sanctuary for birds, butterflies and bees.

This book, brought to you by the editors of *Birds & Blooms* magazine, can serve as your guide to attracting new visitors to your landscape. *Birds & Blooms* has helped lead the trend we like to call "gardening with a purpose" for over 20 years. We've always recognized the importance of going beyond just the beauty of a garden, and purposefully choosing flowers, trees and shrubs for their environmental benefits.

CREATE HABITAT

If you want to create a wildlife-friendly backyard, you must keep three basics in mind: food, water and shelter. Plants are key, but you can also add birdbaths, feeders and nest boxes.

We even went a step further and put together some handy symbols to help you achieve the wildlife-friendly backyard of your dreams. Look for the symbols next to each plant profile to discover what the plant will attract. (Some plants are a triple whammy and attract birds, butterflies and bees!) For extra guidance, check the light-requirement symbols. You'll be able to quickly see if a plant should be grown in shade, part shade or full sun—vital info you need to know to create a great habitat.

Once you've established a flourishing backyard, be sure to enjoy your new guests. Throughout this book, we've highlighted over 60 bird species and 34 butterfly species you might see in your space. Have fun identifying all of the birds, butterflies *and* bees in your own backyard!

Female ruby-throated hummingbird and monarch at butterfly bush

key

🐦 Bird
🐝 Bee
🦋 Butterfly

☀ Full sun
⛅ Part shade
☁ Shade

Question mark on butterfly bush

American goldfinch on sunflower

Mountain bluebird at
purple coneflowers

CHAPTER ONE
Create a Wildlife-Friendly Backyard

Native plants
like purple
coneflowers
and black-eyed
Susans are
the best for
attracting birds.

Serviceberry trees attract many birds, like this male indigo bunting.

Male goldfinch on black-eyed Susan

🐦 Gardening for Birds

It's no secret that you can successfully attract birds with feeders, but what birds need even more than feeders full of seed comes straight from nature: plants and trees. That doesn't mean you shouldn't keep those feeders full, though! But going the extra mile to attract birds with plants and trees will reward you with even more feathered visitors.

Native plants are key, because they'll keep the birds coming back to backyards for more. Berries and seeds bring in more bluebirds, orioles, goldfinches and a whole long list of other most-wanted species. For example, goldfinches often arrive as soon as the first few seeds mature, even while the plant is still in bloom. They'll keep returning in the coming weeks, joined by native sparrows, woodpeckers, juncos, cardinals, chickadees and more.

Junipers provide safe nesting for birds like this yellow-billed cuckoo.

Choose Natives

When it comes to food offerings, seeds and berries are probably the most obvious, but birds are also drawn to something else on the plants that we may never even notice: insects. And the ultimate insect trump card? Caterpillars.

Caterpillars are crucial because they're a prime target for parent birds who have to satisfy a nest full of begging beaks. Birds will eat berries and seeds from nonnative plants, but caterpillars are super finicky and mainly feed on all-American trees, shrubs and flowers. The birds are more than happy to pluck these chubby crawlers from host plants like red-twig dogwood, blueberries and spicebush.

Insects aside, native plants also serve as building supply stores for birds. To make their nests, birds collect twigs and dead leaves or needles from trees and shrubs, and strip fibers and bark from milkweed, Indian hemp, wild grapevines and other natives.

Native plants form symbiotic bonds with birds. The birds get a bounty of food and in return spread seeds to sprout into new plants. But natives are a big win for gardeners, too. They are generally hardy, dependable and low-maintenance and require no coddling to thrive.

Lately, "native" has become something of a buzzword, splashed across just about any plant that originated in North America, which isn't very helpful, because many natives are highly particular about where they'll grow. The saw palmetto of Florida is an American native, but it's not going to be happy in Minnesota and Minnesota's balsam fir definitely won't feel at home in Florida.

If you're just getting started planting natives for birds, daisies are a good choice for beginners, because each flower holds scores of seeds for foraging gold-finches and other friends. All-American native daisies include sunflowers, native asters, coneflowers and black-eyed Susans. (But avoid Goldsturm, a variety of black-eyed Susan that rarely sets seed.) All are top targets of seed-loving birds.

Unless you know what's native to your region, look for widespread natives, those that naturally grow across a big swath of North America. Adaptable enough to flourish in a variety of soils and conditions, they're a good bet for most gardens.

The native serviceberry is a popular choice for cedar waxwings.

12 Common Natives

Widespread in their natural range, these natives easily adapt to life in a garden.

1 ASTERS: many native perennial species, such as calico aster, heart-leaved aster, New England aster, sky blue aster, smooth aster, white wood aster

2 BLACK-EYED SUSANS: short-lived *Rudbeckia hirta,* including the rustic-colored mix known as Gloriosa daisy, and perennial *R. fulgida*

3 BLUE ANISE HYSSOP: *Agastache foeniculum*

4 BROWN-EYED SUSAN *Rudbeckia triloba*

5 CALLIOPSIS: *Coreopsis tinctoria*

6 FIREWHEEL OR INDIAN BLANKET: *Gaillardia* spp.

7 LIATRIS

8 LUPINES: many native species, such as the famous Texas bluebonnet

9 MEXICAN HAT: *Ratibida columnifera*

10 PURPLE CONEFLOWER: *Echinacea purpurea*

11 SUNFLOWERS: annuals and perennials, *Helianthus,* all species

12 YELLOW CONEFLOWER: *Ratibida pinnata*

A garden full of wildlife-friendly plants, bird feeders and shelter for nesters is a winning combination.

Grow Berry Plants

Another secret to a bird-friendly native garden is to have a mix of seed plants and berries. Native berries attract our most-wanted bird friends, including many that aren't backyard feeder regulars. Bluebirds, thrushes, rose-breasted grosbeaks, tanagers, orioles, thrashers, vireos, wood warblers, cedar waxwings, great crested flycatchers—more than 100 species—may visit as soon as the crop begins to ripen.

Plant a hedge of elderberries, dot a solid wall of arborvitae with winterberries, add a serviceberry or flowering dogwood to your flowerbeds, and slip in some blueberries among the azaleas. The downside of planting native berries is that, though it works like a charm, the berries vanish in a hurry. Birds strip berries fast—often in just a few weeks!

Even when they're young, native oaks, maples, ashes, hackberries, black cherries and other large trees attract birds to their sheltering branches and the insects that take up residence on them. Several years down the road, their nuts, seeds or fruit will bring in the birds big-time. Add trees to your yard if you have the space and enjoy the benefits.

With hundreds of natives to choose from in any area, how do you whittle down the selection? Go for those with the greatest appeal—to both you and the birds. If you're looking for a fast payoff, focus on native shrubs and small trees for berries, and flowers for seeds.

Bullock's orioles feed on berries like this graythorn.

Mulberries are tempting to rose-breasted grosbeaks.

Gardening for Butterflies

If you have attracting butterflies on the brain, it's easy to turn your yard into a nonstop butterfly bonanza. When it comes to these fliers, it really is as simple as: "If you build it, they will come." The best butterfly gardens take a little planning but are mostly self-sufficient once they're up and blooming.

You might think of open sunny meadows when you think of butterflies, but don't worry if you only have a small space. A butterfly garden can be as small as a few pots on your back porch, or as large as your whole yard. Include some shady spots if possible—some butterflies prefer it. Remember that the best butterfly gardens can sometimes look a little overgrown or ragged, so don't expect to make this a formal focal point if a pristine garden is important to you.

Red admiral

Great spangled fritillary on purple coneflower

Garden phlox will attract birds and butterflies (like these monarchs).

Plant Butterfly Food Sources

Most butterflies get the majority of their diet from nectar-producing plants, so these should make up the largest part of your garden. Choose native plants when possible, because natives will thrive with little care and often draw the most butterflies. Anchor your garden with a few larger nectar-producing shrubs and add groupings of flowering plants in a variety of colors, heights and flower sizes. Be sure to choose plants that flower in early spring as well as late fall—times when butterflies sometimes struggle to find food.

Your local extension office can provide a list of the best nectar plants for your area, but good bets for almost anyone include salvia, lantana, pentas, aster, marigold, zinnia and coneflower. Buddleia, also known as butterfly bush, can be a good choice in some areas, but make sure it's not considered invasive before you plant.

Not all butterflies rely on nectar plants. Some, like mourning cloaks and red-spotted purples, actually prefer to feed on tree sap or rotting fruit. You can offer fruit like bananas, strawberries and oranges for these butterflies. Keep ants away by filling a shallow dish with water and setting the fruit in the middle.

Eastern tiger swallowtail on purple coneflower

Giant swallowtail
on coneflowers

Provide Water and Shelter

Butterflies get most of the water they need from nectar, but not all. They use their delicate probos- cises to sip water from dewdrops and puddles. Some butterflies, like sulphurs and tiger swallowtails, are especially inclined to gather in large numbers around muddy areas. (The mud provides much-needed salt.) Mimic these natural water areas with a shallow dish of wet sand or mud, or spray down your garden with a fine mist to provide water droplets on the plants.

Butterflies are small and fragile creatures. Raindrops can seem more like bowling balls to them, so when bad weather threatens, butterflies seek shelter. They also need places to roost overnight. Though you can buy ready-made butterfly houses, you'll find butterflies are more likely to use natural areas like tall grasses and thick shrubs. Some butter- flies even overwinter in crevices inside tree bark and rocks. Others spend the winter as caterpillars or chrysalides buried deep in the leaf litter beneath trees, so don't be too quick to remove all that fallen foliage each autumn.

The Importance of Host Plants

Any legitimate wildlife garden provides a place for creatures to raise their young. While butterflies are anything but dutiful parents—they lay their eggs and then leave the young caterpillars to fend for them- selves—they do need places to deposit their eggs. Every butterfly species has a plant or group of plants that their caterpillars will eat, known as host plants. The best way to attract a wider variety of butterflies is to provide the host plants they need. Just remember that the purpose of these plants is to feed caterpillars, so the plants will get chewed up and defoliated. For once, holes in the leaves mean gardeners are doing something right!

To determine the best host plants for your garden, start by finding out which butterflies are regular visitors to your area. Once again, extension offices or local butterfly gardens are a great source of information. Then start seeking out the host plants these butterflies need. They are almost always native plants, and more often than not, they're what others might consider weeds. No good butterfly garden can do without them, though, so choose those that best suit your site and plant as many as you possibly can.

Host plants vary by area, but nearly anyone can plant milkweed for monarchs, hollyhocks for painted ladies and violets for great spangled fritillaries. Some butterfly and moth caterpillars use trees, too, so if you have space, consider adding ash or willow for tiger swallowtails and mourning cloaks.

To get the most out of your butterfly garden, observe the space at different times of day. In the morning, butterflies are a little slow to get started, especially if the air is cooler, so it's a wonderful time to take photos. Sunny afternoons bring out butterflies in high numbers, and evenings are the time to enjoy beautiful moths. Take time to hunt for caterpillars, too, and buy a good field guide to learn what to look for. Most of all, find a little time each day to sit quietly and watch your winged visitors come and go.

11 Backyard Host Plant Picks

Aster *Aster*
Birch *Betula*
Sunflower *Helianthus*
Lupine *Lupinus*
Crabapple *Malus*
Poplar *Ponulus*
Cherry *Prunus*
Oak *Quercus*
Willow *Salix*
Goldenrod *Solidago*
Milkweed *Asclepias*

Sunflowers attract several butterfly species, including swallowtails, checkerspots and painted ladies.

Bumblebee

🐝 Gardening for Bees and Other Insects

In order to create a yard that's safe and attractive to native bees, it's important to understand these fascinating creatures. A few of their behaviors might surprise you, and knowing these things will help you grow a garden fit for these powerful pollinators.

First and foremost, you might not even realize they're there. Native bees can look different from how we often visualize these flying insects. They actually exist in an array of colors, including metallic green, brown, black and gray, as well as the stereotypical yellow-and-black stripes. Native bees can be quite small and are often mistaken for flies. It's also useful to note that native bees tend to be docile. Most bees cannot sting humans.

Another common misconception about bees is where they nest. Most solitary bee species nest in the ground; the rest use tunnels like hollow stems or burrow into dead wood. Inside these nesting sites, the female bee creates a pollen loaf, lays a single egg on it, then starts a new nesting site and repeats the process. To create a safe habitat for this type of nesting, it's essential to have areas of undisturbed, loose ground. Bees tend to select south-facing slopes with well-drained soil, which can be warmer

and drier, and make for good nesting sites. If you genuinely want to attract nesting bees, think about forgoing mulch. A lot of native bees are too small to get through the mulch layer.

When cutting back your plants in fall, leave behind foot-long lengths of pithy or hollow stems for the tunnel nesters. Cavity-nesting bees will also use those stems the next year. You can also create natural bee houses by bundling together hollow stems and hanging them in the yard. Fallen wood, brush piles or old fence posts also provide good nesting sites.

You know the term "busy bee?" Well, it couldn't be more true—native bees are extremely busy. Most female native bees are active as adults for two to six weeks. During that time, they are collecting pollen to create as many loaves and lay as many eggs as possible. To make foraging for pollen less arduous, provide a diverse selection of flowers from spring to fall and plant them in groups.

New generations and different species of bees are emerging throughout the growing season and it's essential that they have enough flowers for pollen collection. Gardeners should identify flowering gaps during the growing season and add plants to the yard accordingly, so that bees can get a continuous succession of flowering plants.

A Bee or Not a Bee?

Just because it buzzes doesn't mean it's a bee. You may be surprised to learn just how many other garden bugs masquerade as bees, including moths, beetles and the real masters of disguise, flies. Although usually considered pests, flies are big allies in the yard and garden. These bee look-alikes really are good bugs for your garden.

The most common bee mimics are the hoverflies, members of the Syrphidae family, which resemble small bees or wasps like yellow jackets. Some even sound like wasps, with the frequency of their wing beats matching that of their stinging counterparts. They are garden friendly, helping to pollinate flowers and eat aphids.

The Asilidae family's robber flies are excellent mimics of bumblebees. Instead of visiting flowers, they perch on foliage, twigs or the ground, and then scan the sky overhead. When another insect flies over, the robber fly zooms off to grab the victim and then returns to its perch. This fly family also helps control some of the less desirable garden insects.

Bee flies, sometimes called "wanna-bees," are in the Bombyliidae family. Their hairy bodies are delicate and can go bald quickly during their brief lives as adults. Many bee flies have a long proboscis that looks much like a mosquito's bloodsucking snout.

No worries, though—bee flies are harmless and feed on flower nectar.

Feather-legged flies in the Tachinidae family really take their disguise to the next level with fake pollen baskets on their hind legs. As adults, they may pollinate flowers; as larvae, they are parasitic on stinkbugs and squash bugs. These flies are certainly good bugs for your garden!

So, after all of that, how do you tell if it's a bee or a fly? Look for these characteristics and don't be afraid to get close. Foraging bees are too intent on what they're doing to bother with you, and flies have no stingers at all.

Wings: Bees have two pairs of wings, whereas flies have only one set. But since the forewings and hind wings of bees are usually connected, they may appear to have only one pair.

Antennae: Bees have relatively long antennae. Most flies have very short antennae, with a long bristle called an arista at the tip.

Eyes: Both bees and flies have compound eyes that excel at detecting motion, which is why it's so hard to swat them. But flies, unlike bees, have enormous eyes that meet at the top of the head in the male, and nearly so in the female.

Mouthparts: Bees have chewing mouthparts and a tonguelike proboscis. Flies have a spongy pad at the end of a flexible "arm," or a spearlike beak.

Behavior: Few bees hover, at least for extended periods. Many flies seem to be able to hover indefinitely.

Sweat bee

Bee Garden Basics

When gardening for bees, here are a few general rules of thumb:

- Choose a range of flower shapes and colors to attract the most bee species. Bumblebees can easily collect pollen from complex flowers, while smaller bees appreciate simple flower shapes and a flat place to land.

- Plant season-long blooms to support bees from early spring until fall.

- Provide areas of undisturbed ground or vegetation for nesting sites.

- Bees and flowers have evolved in tandem, so make sure to choose nonhybrid natives.

- Plant in masses for efficient pollen collection. Sunny areas are most attractive.

- Avoid pesticide use. Even some organic mixtures can harm insects.

- Provide a muddy area or shallow trough for water.

Pansies

CHAPTER TWO Annuals

▲ BACHELOR'S BUTTON
Centaurea cyanus

Growing best in full sun, bachelor's button comes in several colors, including blue, pink, red, white and purple. Though considered an annual, its seeds ensure a new crop each year. Butterflies will visit for nectar, and in fall, finches, buntings and sparrows will stop by to nibble from the seed heads. Also known as cornflower, this charmer is long-lasting when cut and holds its color when dried.

▼ BEGONIA
Begonia spp., Annual to Zone 10

For a metallic-leafed begonia, like Metallic Mist, look to the Rex and rhizomatous varieties. This shade-lover adds hints of silver to borders and hanging baskets.

DID YOU KNOW?
Borage is not only pretty, but it's a great plant for dry areas.

▲ BORAGE
Borago officinalis

The clear blue star-shaped flowers of borage stand out in the garden. You can eat the cucumber-flavored leaves raw, steamed or sautéed. This annual self-seeds, so it will be a long-lasting member of the garden. And you will have plenty of seedlings to share with family and friends!

► BROCCOLI
Brassica oleracea italica

 |

A host plant for cabbage white butterfly larvae, broccoli also attracts the birds that feed on the caterpillars. This member of the cabbage family is ready to eat about two months after planting.

CALENDULA
Calendula officinalis

You may also know this edible flower as pot marigold. The yellowish white and orange petals were once used to flavor soups and stews. Grow in full sun with moist, well-drained soil. It thrives in cooler temperatures.

▲ CALIBRACHOA
Calibrachoa spp.

Its small petunialike flowers will steal the show all season, making fast-growing calibrachoa a hot choice for beds and containers—especially those that are geared toward butterflies and hummingbirds. Use it as a nicely textured filler plant or as a bold stand-alone. Plants reach about 8 inches tall and spread to about 1 foot wide.

▶ CARROT
Daucus carota **var.** *sativus*

It's not the crunchy orange spikes that entice black swallowtail caterpillars, it's the tops. Plant the tiny seeds in loose, well-draining soil for best results—and if you want long, straight carrots, be sure the soil is rock-free, too.

CELOSIA
Celosia argentea

This velvety favorite doesn't mind heat, so get it going in summer and it will last well into autumn. Available in shades of red, purple, orange and yellow, celosia plants have two different types of flower heads: feathered and spiky, or wavy and flat. The latter resembles a rooster's comb, hence this long-lasting flower's other name, cockscomb. Celosia can thrive in a wide range of soils, including heavy clay.

Cosmos

▲ CLEOME
Cleome hassleriana

Plant this tropical native in your garden and you're sure to attract attention. This bloom, which some call spider flower, is a top nectar source for swallowtail butterflies and hummingbirds. Cleome's tall stems, topped by wispy pink, purple or white flowers, are hard to miss. Plants tend to reseed themselves from one year to the next if goldfinches don't get to them first!

COSMOS
Cosmos spp.

Throughout the growing season, birds and butterflies can't resist these colorful, pinwheel-shaped blossoms with feathery foliage. Grow single or double cultivars of this easygoing bloomer in full sun, and you'll have flowers and seeds from summer through late fall. Plants stand from 1 to 6 feet high, so no matter how large your space, there's a type of cosmos that will fit right in.

▶ DILL
Anethum graveolens

Don't be surprised if you see black swallowtails flitting among dill's green fronds. This herb is a larval host plant. In summer and fall, yellow blooms open on broad flower heads. At 3 to 4 feet tall, dill sometimes needs to be staked. It thrives in well-draining, sandy or loamy soil.

▲ FENNEL
Foeniculum vulgare

With a dill-like top and stems that resemble celery, you could assume fennel tastes like a cross between the two. Nope! Instead, think licorice. Attractive to butterflies and other beneficial insects, as well as songbirds, fennel reaches about 3 feet tall and prefers rich, well-draining soil.

◄ FLOSS FLOWER
Ageratum houstonianum

Floss flower's fuzzy clusters make soft landing pads for hungry butterflies. This fast-growing plant, also known as ageratum, is common in sunny garden borders and containers thanks to its compact size: a petite 6 to 12 inches. Purple, pink, blue or white blooms beckon fliers-by.

◄ FLOWERING TOBACCO
Nicotiana spp.

For a no-fuss way to liven up your garden, plant flowering tobacco! Ranging from 10 inches to 5 feet high, the stems are covered with star-shaped flowers in shades of red, maroon, lavender, white, pink, yellow and even green. Some types, including members of the *N. sylvestris* species, have a lovely scent, especially in the evening.

▼ FOUR-O'CLOCKS
Mirabilis jalapa, Annual to Zone 10

Almost like clockwork, this often fragrant flower blooms in late afternoon. Each blossom lives for just one day, fading before noon. Flowers are available in yellow, pink, purple, red, white and lavender—sometimes on the same plant. Additional varieties, like the Jingles mix, are striped.

DID YOU KNOW?
You can enjoy geraniums indoors, too! Snip off some blooms and add them to your own flower bouquet.

▲ **FUCHSIA**
Fuchsia spp., Annual to Zone 8

Fuchsia's showy, pendulous red, white, pink and purple blooms will capture your heart. There are more than 100 kinds, from low-growing dwarfs and trailing plants to upright shrubs. Fuchsia grows best in moist soil and partial shade, so it's ideal for attracting hummingbirds to less-than-sunny yards. Fertilize weekly for best results.

▶ **GERANIUM**
Pelargonium

It's up for debate, but the geranium may be known and loved by more people than any other flower in the world. The plant's vivid colors and long-lasting blossoms make it a favorite for backyards everywhere, flowering from summer to frost. Multicolored Peppermint Twist is eye-catching. If you'd rather have a solid, the Orbit series has a glowing red variety.

▼ HELIOTROPE
Heliotropium arborescens

🦋 🐝 | ⛅ ☀️

Heliotrope's fruity scent has earned it the nickname cherry pie. Its compact growth habit and profuse purplish blooms make it a good choice for containers and flower beds. Plants reach 2 feet tall and up to 15 inches wide. Watch yours for all types of butterflies, from blues to monarchs.

▲ IMPATIENS
Impatiens spp.

🐦 🦋 | ☁️ ⛅ ☀️

Invite winged creatures into the shade with impatiens. Sparrows, finches, grosbeaks and buntings eat the seeds, while hummingbirds and butterflies drop in for a sip of nectar. Growing 6 inches to 2 feet high, impatiens has a mounding growth habit, making it a good choice for borders, foundation beds and containers.

▶ LANTANA
Lantana camara, Annual to Zone 9

🐦 🦋 | ☀️

With its abundant clusters of tiny, nectar-rich flowers, why wouldn't hummingbirds and butterflies, including swallowtails and hairstreaks, love lantana? Later in the growing season, birds nibble its berries, as well. In more tropical climates, lantana is grown as a shrub and can become invasive. With a mounding or trailing habit, smaller varieties work well in containers.

▲ MARIGOLD
Tagetes spp.

  | ☀

A tough yet easygoing plant, this old-fashioned favorite flowers all summer. With many bloom styles and heights to choose from, you're bound to find the perfect marigold for any sunny space. The Queen Sophia cultivar sports two shades of orange on each ruffly bloom.

▶ MEXICAN BUSH SAGE
Salvia leucantha, Annual to Zone 8

  | ☀

Butterflies and hummingbirds will be clamoring for a space at this plant's late-blooming purplish flowers. In areas where this sage is hardy, it can be established as a shrub. In cooler zones, plant it outdoors as soon as the threat of frost has passed: It needs a long growing season. No matter where you live, grow Mexican bush sage in full sun with moist yet well-draining soil.

4 Warm-Colored Plants

Adding warm shades to your garden, among pinks and purples, will make you feel happy and energized.

Black-eyed Susan
Poppies
Zinnias
Mexican sunflowers

▲ **MEXICAN SUNFLOWER**
Tithonia rotundifolia

This fast-growing annual, which blooms in late summer and autumn, reaches 6 feet in height. Its long-lasting orange and red flowers glow in full sun. For smaller spaces, try a compact variety such as Goldfinger or Fiesta Del Sol. Resist the urge to deadhead—songbirds enjoy the seeds.

◄ NASTURTIUM
Tropaeolum spp.

Humans aren't the only ones who enjoy nasturtiums: Moth and butterfly caterpillars like to munch on its leaves, as do some songbirds. The nectar attracts many types of fliers. Once it's established, nasturtium performs best when left alone, contributing vivid color all season long. Some types grow in mounds, while others are good climbers.

PANSY
Viola x *wittrockiana*

This colorful flower is best known for the whiskered "faces" that mark many of the blooms. The majority of pansies are annuals, though some live longer. Most perform best in cooler weather, so in warm climates they're valued for bringing much-needed color to dull winter landscapes.

▼ PARSLEY
Petroselinum crispum

It's a must for herb gardens and butterfly gardens, too, since parsley is a host plant for the black swallowtail. With curly or flat leaves, it prefers cooler temperatures and grows best in full sun and slightly acidic soil.

Pansy

▲ PENTAS
Pentas lanceolata

Also called star clusters, these tropical beauties are a natural choice for butterfly gardens. Pentas are found in many colors, from deep red to white, and make excellent nectar plants. Grow this flower, in varieties ranging from 8 inches to 3 feet high, in full sun or part shade.

▶ PETUNIA
Petunia x hybrida

If you love petunias but are on the lookout for something a little different, Black Velvet is perfect for you. Petunias have long been used in hanging baskets to attract hummingbirds, and this one will do that with a dash of drama.

PURPLETOP VERVAIN
Verbena bonariensis, Annual to Zone 7

🦋 | ☀️

Entice fall-flying butterflies with these delicate, long-stemmed purple flowers. People will take notice, too. This plant can grow up to 5 feet tall. Check with your local extension office before planting because it's invasive in some areas.

◄ SALVIA
Salvia splendens

Also known as firecracker plant, this annual variety of salvia pops in any garden, producing season-long color in just about any landscape. Depending on the cultivar, this annual will reach 8 inches to 2 feet, though newer varieties are on the compact side.

▼ SNAPDRAGON
Antirrhinum majus

Despite the intimidating name, butterflies (including common buckeye caterpillars) love the snapdragon. It's easily recognized by its distinctive overlapping petals, which come in appealing hues of pink, red, yellow, orange, white, purple and bronze, plus bicolors. Though it usually blooms throughout the growing season, snapdragon is most floriferous when temperatures are cooler.

◄ SUNFLOWER
Helianthus annuus

   |

There's something about a sunflower's bright face that simply makes you feel good. And when it comes to kids, few plants cause more excitement than these towering blooms, which can soar up to 15 feet! Tiny nectar-producing flower clusters make up the center, attracting butterflies and hummers. It's no secret that the seeds are a favorite among backyard birds.

9 Bird-Friendly Sunflowers

Strawberry Blonde
Mammoth Russian
Italian White
Little Becka
Moulin Rouge
Soraya
Lemon Queen
Super Snack Mix
Taiyo Sunflower

◄ SWEET PEA
Lathyrus odoratus

 |

This fragrant flower is easy to grow and provides flowers for cutting all season long. Like edible peas, sweet pea prefers the cooler weather of spring and early summer, gradually declining in the heat of August. A few cultivars, including the Royal and Old Spice mixes, are exceptionally heat-tolerant.

▲ VERBENA
Verbena x hybrida, Annual to Zone 9

 | ☀

Expect summerlong color from these attractive blooms. The plant's stems spread out to about 18 inches. Keep the soil moist but well drained for optimal flowering.

◄ VIOLA
Viola cornuta

 | ☁ ☀

Also known as the horned violet, the faintly scented, low-maintenance viola tolerates sun and partial shade. It blooms most profusely in cool weather, when it's an ideal nectar source for cabbage whites, sulphurs, blues and others. Increase insect traffic to your garden by planting these low growers at the base of taller nectar sources.

ZINNIA
Zinnia spp.

A hummingbird and butterfly garden go-to, several varieties of sparrows, finches and juncos eat seeds later in the year. It reaches up to 3 feet and blooms until the first frost.

Alliums

CHAPTER THREE Perennials

AGASTACHE
Agastache spp., Zones 4 to 11

Bushy and studded with blooms from mid- to late summer, agastache is a favorite of hummingbirds, butterflies and bees. Flower spires in violet, orange, yellow, pink or blue reach 2 to 6 feet high. Agastache thrives in full sun and in well-draining, fertile soil.

▲ ALLIUM
Allium spp., Zones 2 to 10

 |

Looking to add a colorful bounce to your garden? There's no better bloomer than allium! This pretty perennial is a winning selection, available in shades of purple, pink, white and yellow. Not only can you find an allium to suit nearly any spot, this enchanting plant is easy to grow, and different species bloom from midspring until fall.

◄ ALPINE SPEEDWELL
Veronica allionii, Zones 2 to 9

 |

Like its larger cousins, this compact speedwell features chubby spikes that flower over an olive-green cushion of foliage. Because it's a low grower, you'll find it works wonderfully in feature spots like borders.

► ANISE HYSSOP
Agastache foeniculum, Zones 4 to 11

 |

This North American native produces spikes of blue flowers above anise-scented leaves in late summer. The plants grow 3 feet tall, self-seed and tolerate drought once they're established. Be sure to deadhead to encourage more blooms.

▼ APPLE
Malus spp., Zones 3 to 8

The apple is cultivated across North America for its pretty spring flowers and tasty late-season fruit. It's a host to the white admiral. Grosbeaks nibble the flower buds and robins, thrushes and others flock for the fruit. It prefers moist but well-draining soil and full sun.

▲ ASTER
Aster spp., Zones 3 to 8

 |

A popular cut flower, the aster incites an explosion of color to the end of the growing season. From miniature alpine plants to giants that tower up to 6 feet, asters will brighten fall, especially when the late-season butterflies come to visit. Hundreds of varieties give gardeners plenty of options.

▶ ASTILBE
Astilbe spp., Zones 4 to 9

 |

Its fernlike appearance helps astilbe fit right into a shade garden—though its flower spikes, which grow from about 1 to 4 feet tall, can't help but steal the spotlight. For a touch of glamour, try Bridal Veil. From afar, the flowers on this and some other astilbe varieties look like feathers.

◀ BAPTISIA
Baptisia spp., Zones 3 to 9

  |

In early summer, this North American native's stems are laden with small flowers that later form structural seed heads sought after by birds. Select from a variety of colors, cultivars and hybrids to find the perfect plant for your space. Plant baptisia with ample room in a place where you won't have to move it: It develops a deep taproot and is finicky about being transplanted.

▼ BEE BALM
Monarda spp., Zones 3 to 9

 | ☀

Also known as bergamot, this unusual beauty grows up to 4 feet tall and starts flowering in midsummer, inviting hummingbirds, butterflies and bees to your flower bed. Plants come in hues of pinkx, red, white and purple; choose mildew-resistant varieties for best results. Frequent deadheading will keep this enthusiastic self-sower in check, but then you won't see songbirds stopping to eat the seeds once petals die back. The choice is yours!

DID YOU KNOW?
Plants like bee balm, bachelor's button and cosmos not only lure helpful insects that will prey upon damaging insects, but also attract pollinators.

▶ BELLFLOWER

Campanula spp., Zones 3 to 9

This dainty plant, available in annual, perennial and biennial cultivars, enjoys moist soil and thrives in full sun to partial shade. In late spring and early summer, it unveils bell-shaped flowers in colors ranging from blue to purple to white. Some varieties, like the Serbian bellflower, have long-lasting blooms and evergreen foliage in Zones 8 and 9.

▼ BLACK-EYED SUSAN

Rudbeckia spp., Zones 3 to 9

Lovely as a background planting or in a wildflower garden, black-eyed Susan also shines when grouped with other daisy-shaped flowers. Plants range from 1 to 6 feet in height, offering a big visual impact in any size yard. Birds love the late-fall seed heads.

▲ BLANKET FLOWER
Gaillardia spp., Zones 3 to 10

Not only is blanket flower bright and cheery, it's one tough plant. Tolerant of drought and a variety of soil conditions, this North American native, sometimes grown as an annual, is a standout in any sunny spot. At the end of the growing season, you can save and dry the seeds and plant them the following spring.

▶ BLAZING STAR
Liatris spp., Zones 3 to 9

The nectar of this spiky plant is a butterfly favorite, especially when it comes to the silver-spotted skipper. After the flowers fade, birds favor the seeds, which are easy to pick out in the garden—plants reach up to 6 feet tall! Some types, like Kobold, are much shorter, measuring roughly 18 inches.

Bleeding heart

▲ BLEEDING HEART
Dicentra spectabilis, Zones 3 to 9

Give life to a shady spot by planting a few of these delicate perennials. Long-lasting blooms open in midspring, covering this graceful plant with gorgeous floral pendants in shades of rose pink and creamy white. Watch for a hummingbird or two hovering nearby.

◂ BLUEBERRY

Vaccinium spp., Zones 3 to 10

Producing bell-shaped white flowers in spring and plump, flavorful fruits in summer, this shrub supplies food for butterflies, birds, small mammals and humans. The blueberry is a plant for all seasons. Green leaves turn to orange or red in autumn, and the bright stems are attractive through winter. Just be sure to select a species suited for your region.

BUTTERFLY WEED

Asclepias tuberosa, Zones 3 to 9

Not solely a treat for butterflies, this drought-tolerant plant is a wildlife garden must-have. Its foliage is the food of larval monarch and queen butterflies, while hummingbirds love the flat-topped flower clusters' nectar and birds, such as goldfinches and orioles, use the silky down of spent seed pods as nesting material. Despite its name, it's far from being a pest.

▾ CARDINAL FLOWER

Lobelia cardinalis, Zones 3 to 9

A moisture-loving favorite, bright-red cardinal flower grows 3 to 5 feet tall and blooms for most of summer and into autumn. It does well when planted in full sun to partial shade and fertile, moist soil. Hummingbirds and butterflies (especially those in the swallowtail family) seek out this plant's nectar, but don't expect to see cardinals hanging around nearby—the flower is named merely for the color.

Butterfly weed

CANDYTUFT

Iberis sempervirens, Zones 5 to 9

Roll out the white carpet for your garden with this dense mat of pale blooms perfect for borders, rock gardens or containers. Clusters of flowers bloom from spring into summer, leaving candytuft's evergreen foliage to maintain interest all year through.

◄ CATMINT
Nepeta x *faassenii*, Zones 3 to 8

Don't let the name sway you from planting this bee favorite. Look for well-behaved varieties that do not reseed and take over the garden. You and the bees will be rewarded with blue flowers that top silvery foliage all season long.

▼ CHRYSANTHEMUM
Chrysanthemum and Dendranthema, Zones 4 to 8

Mum's the word for many gardeners in autumn, and with good reason. The chrysanthemum is prized for painting landscapes with dense, vivid color, and its excellent frost tolerance ensures a long and lovely show. When planted in spring or summer, this shrubby tender perennial is often called a hardy mum, because it has time to become established. Planted in fall, mums are grown as annuals.

▲ COLUMBINE
Aquilegia spp., Zones 3 to 9

Blooming exuberantly from spring to early summer, columbine's distinctive flowers come in a wide spectrum of solids and bicolors, boasting single or double sets of petals. Plants range from 8 inches to 3 feet high. Watch for all sorts of pollinators, plus the aptly named columbine duskywing butterfly, which uses this as a host plant.

▶ COMMON BUGLEWEED
Ajuga reptans, Zones 3 to 9

This evergreen perennial makes an excellent ground cover with its masses of bronze, green or variegated foliage. Columns of blue or pink flowers appear in spring and early summer, inviting butterflies and newly arrived hummingbirds to sip its nectar. Deer-resistant bugleweed is an aggressive grower and may invade lawns, so plant yours within a barrier. On the upside, you won't have to wait long for it to fill in after planting!

10 Bird-Friendly Coneflowers

Sunrise
Pink Double Delight
Virgin
Raspberry Truffle
Green Envy
Tangerine Dream
Powwow Wild Berry
Sombrero Salsa Red
Magnus Superior
Green Jewel

CONEFLOWER
Echinacea spp., Zones 3 to 9

Birds, bees and butterflies, such as fritillaries, truly love this perennial! You'll see songbirds pause to nibble the seeds, and butterflies and hummers stopping for its nectar into fall. In winter, the remaining seed heads leave an interesting garden focal point.

▶ CORAL BELLS
Heuchera sanguinea, Zones 3 to 8

Wands of primarily red bell-shaped flowers and handsome, sometimes evergreen, foliage make this bloomer a valuable addition to any garden, whether it's located in a sunny or shady spot. This adaptable mounding plant is a striking border or container plant and will increase hummingbird traffic in your yard. To extend coral bells' blooming season, clip off spent stems.

COREOPSIS
Coreopsis spp., Zones 3 to 11

Though you can find annual varieties of this graceful plant that's easy to grow from seed, make sure you pick up one of the perennial versions, too. It loves the sun and grows well in dry conditions. A rainbow of new varieties offers striking alternatives to the traditional yellow blooms. Plants range from 8 to 48 inches in height. After the butterfly attracting flowers fade, songbirds eat the seeds.

▼ CREEPING PHLOX
Phlox subulata, Zones 3 to 8

Topping off at just 6 inches, creeping phlox is a smaller, mat-forming relative of the familiar fragrant perennial. When it blooms in spring, it forms a carpet of pretty little blossoms that entice passing butterflies. When nestled into a protective layer of mulch, creeping phlox doesn't require much watering.

Coral Bells for Hummingbirds

Dolce Blackberry Ice	Green Spice
Berry Smoothie	Midnight Rose
Citronelle	Amber Waves
Peppermint Spice	Hollywood

Coreopsis

◄ CROCOSMIA

Crocosmia spp., Zones 5 to 9

This dramatic hummingbird magnet reaches 3 feet high, unfurling wiry stems of bright blossoms from mid- to late summer. Moist soil is important for optimal flowering. Crocosmia makes an excellent cut flower and adds tropical flair to any space, outdoors or in. But be warned: It's invasive in some areas.

▶ CROCUS

Crocus, Zones 3 to 8

Start off spring with a burst of color in the landscape and nectar for the bees. Grow these small early bloomers in full sun or partial shade. Planting crocus in bulk will make an even greater impact in the garden.

DAFFODIL

Narcissus, Zones 2 to 9

Daffodils' sunny trumpets are among the first beacons of spring. They'll grow in most types of soil and don't mind some shade. February Gold is an extra-early bloomer.

Daffodil

DAHLIA
Dahlia spp., Zones 8 to 11

It's no wonder the dahlia is the darling of many gardeners. With thousands of cultivars out there, there are colors, shapes and sizes for everyone. Some varieties easily surpass 5 feet, and the flowers grow as big as dinner plates. Gardeners in cooler climates should dig up the tubers once the plants have died back after frost arrives.

Delphinium

▲ DAYLILY
Hemerocallis, Zones 3 to 10

This summer bloomer is cherished for its reliability and variety. With many thousands of cultivars available, gardeners have almost limitless options. Though the blossoms last just a day, you'll find many hybrids that flower repeatedly all season long.

DELPHINIUM
Delphinium, Zones 3 to 7

This towering treasure makes a statement at the back of a mixed border, as a vertical accent or in a container. With dozens of blooms on each stem, it gives hummingbirds plenty of nectar sources to share with butterflies and other bugs, too.

▶ DIANTHUS
Dianthus, Zones 3 to 10

One of the world's oldest cultivated flowers, dianthus is prized for its ruffled petals, pleasant scent and generous spring and summer blooming period. Ranging from just 4 inches to 36 inches high, dianthus grows well in full sun.

▲ EVENING PRIMROSE
Oenothera, Zones 3 to 9

A good choice for poor or dry soil, warm tones of this spring to summer bloomer attract hummers best. Typically, plants reach heights of 2 to 3 feet and may need support.

◄ EVERLASTING
Anaphalis margaritacea, Zones 3 to 8

Maybe you're more familiar with this plant by its common name pearly everlasting, but its beauty is the same no matter what you call it. Blooming from midsummer to early fall, this plant boasts small, flat-topped clumps of white flowers reaching about 2 feet tall.

FALSE ASTER
Boltonia asteroides, Zones 3 to 9

You might know this plant better as boltonia. Add a natural look to your yard with false aster, a North American native often seen growing in sunny wetlands and along riverbanks. An eye-catching border backdrop, this perennial's flowers have spindly purple, white or pink petals. The gracefully arching plants grow 2 to 6 feet high. You may want to give false aster a haircut each spring to help keep it in shape.

◀ FORGET-ME-NOT
Myosotis sylvatica, Zones 3 to 9

Early-season butterflies remember to visit these dainty blooms, which range from the classic blue to white and pink. Though forget-me-not is considered a biennial, it produces a lot of seeds, making it a smart self-sowing ground cover. Do a little research before planting forget-me-nots because it's invasive in some areas.

▶ FOXGLOVE
Digitalis spp., Zones 3 to 10

With 18-inch to 6-foot spires covered with bright, bell-shaped blooms, this showy plant can't be missed. Self-seeding foxglove is a biennial or short-lived perennial, so leave the spent flowers in place and you'll be treated to a new crop of blooms each spring.

▼ GARDEN PHLOX
Phlox paniculata, Zones 3 to 8

People love the sweet fragrance of this charming classic, but butterflies and hummingbirds visit for the nectar. A tough, reliable plant, garden phlox blooms all summer with a little deadheading. Grow this pretty plant, which can reach up to 3 feet tall, in full sun, and water regularly.

▲ GLOBE THISTLE
Echinops ritro, Zones 3 to 9

 |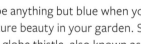

Butterflies will be anything but blue when you plant this spiny-looking azure beauty in your garden. Standing up to 2 feet tall, globe thistle, also known as blue hedgehog, grows best in poor but well-draining soil and full sun. Butterflies, bees and moths relish the nectar, and once seed heads form, finches and other birds will stop by to eat.

▶ GOLDENROD
Solidago spp., Zones 3 to 9

Light up your autumn garden with goldenrod's wispy yellow blooms, which also make long-lasting cut flowers. Choose a type that's not an aggressive self-seeder, such as Fireworks. That way, you won't have to deadhead as often, and the birds will have fortifying seeds to eat when the weather cools.

GRAPE HYACINTH
Muscari, Zones 3 to 9

🦋 | ⛅ ☀️

A hardy spring bulb, grape hyacinth sports cobalt-hued flowers resembling tiny grapes. This plant easily spreads to form a sea of fragrant blue blooms.

 **HOLLYHOCK**
Alcea rosea, Zones 3 to 9

🐦 🦋 🐝 | ☀️

If you want to make an impact in your garden, look no further than this tall host plant to butterfly larvae, including hairstreaks, skippers and painted ladies. It comes in many colors, attracts a variety of insects and hummingbirds and can reach up to 8 feet tall. Hollyhock is a biennial, so it grows foliage on short stems its first year but doesn't flower until the next. From then on, it self-seeds.

HOSTA
Hosta, Zones 3 to 8

The ultimate low-care shade plant, hosta comes in endless varieties and colors. It also can be easily divided—perfect for the budget-minded. Hosta forms a dense, leafy clump, with blossoms rising up to 3 feet above the foliage. Thousands of cultivars offer a wide array of leaf colors, shapes, patterns and textures. While some hostas tolerate sun, those grown in partial shade generally produce the most handsome, longest-lasting foliage.

◀ JAPANESE ANEMONE
Anemone x hybrida, Zones 4 to 8

Well suited to sun or partial shade, the Japanese anemone produces saucer-shaped white or pink flowers throughout the season. Be sure the site you choose to plant it has moist, humus-rich soil and gets some sun. A fine choice for autumn, it thrives in cool, damp conditions.

▼ JOE PYE WEED
Eupatorium spp., Zones 3 to 11

A sun-loving, sky-high perennial that needs no staking, this native wildflower is a showstopper when its giant puffs of mauve florets come into bloom. You can find varieties for smaller spaces, too, such as Little Joe and Gateway.

◀ LAMBS' EARS
Stachys byzantina, Zones 4 to 8

Easily recognized by its woolly, silvery-gray foliage, lambs' ears is a trusty bedding plant and ground cover that also makes a wonderful companion plant. Standing about 18 inches tall, lambs' ears thrives in full sun to partial shade. You can't go wrong with its long growing season: early summer to frost.

▼ LAVENDER
Lavandula spp., Zones 5 to 10

In the summertime, hummingbirds, skippers, painted ladies and other pollinators frequently visit lavender. You'll love this Mediterranean bloomer for its attractive flower spires, silvery-green foliage and calming scent. Varieties of this flower grow from 1 to 4 feet tall, and are available in many shades of purple as well as white and light pink.

▲ LUNGWORT
Pulmonaria spp., Zones 2 to 8

A popular early nectar source for hummingbirds, lungwort's blue, purple, pink or white blooms and dappled leaves lend interest to shady backyards. The foliage often remains green clear into winter, making this plant an all-season asset. Most cultivars are about 12 inches tall and thrive in moist, well-draining soil.

▲ LUPINE
Lupinus spp., Zones 3 to 8

Give your backyard a bit of rustic charm by planting a stand of lupines. With colors and sizes that suit any garden, varieties range from native species to new hybrids. Hummingbirds, butterflies (especially blues) and songbirds all seek out this late-spring bloomer, which prefers sun or partial shade.

▲ **MALTESE CROSS**
Lychnis chalcedonica, Zones 3 to 9

With bold red flowers on a plant 2 to 3 feet high and
1 to 2 feet wide, this bright bloomer will dress up your
summer flower garden. Plant it in fertile, moist,
well-draining soil.

▲ ORIENTAL POPPY
Papaver orientale, Zones 2 to 9

This plant can be difficult to grow, since it doesn't handle transplanting well and requires a sunny site with adequately draining soil. But the oriental poppy's vibrant, papery blooms are worth the effort. In the right location, this exotic-looking flower fills in quickly and rewards gardeners with years of enjoyment.

▼ PASQUE FLOWER
Pulsatilla vulgaris, Zones 4 to 8

An early-spring bloomer, pasque flower adds an element of texture to any garden. While it's likely not a go-to perennial for most gardeners, we think this drought-tolerant, fuss-free flower certainly deserves top honors and some attention.

NEW YORK IRONWEED
Vernonia noveboracensis, Zones 5 to 9

Add rustic charm to your garden with New York ironweed's clouds of purple flowers, which butterflies love. Birds like the autumn seed heads. This North American native blooms in August and September on sturdy, statuesque stems. The adaptable, sun-loving perennial flourishes in any moist to normal soil.

▲ PEAR

Pyrus communis, Zones 3 to 9

A pear tree is a pretty and practical addition to a wildlife garden. Reaching up to 50 feet tall, this tree has lovely spring blooms and autumn foliage. Many types of butterflies—anglewings and admirals—and birds enjoy the fruit.

▲ PENSTEMON

Penstemon spp., Zones 3 to 10

Hummingbirds favor this spiky trumpet-shaped flower, which comes in pink, red, purple, blue and white. Varieties reach heights of up to 4 feet and bloom profusely for most or all of the summer. Full sun and well-draining soil, including the sandy stuff, are ideal.

▶ PINCUSHION FLOWER
Scabiosa spp., Zones 3 to 9

This plant gets its name from the way its stamens stick into the flower head. Whether you choose the annual or perennial variety, 1- to 3-foot-tall pincushion flowers come in purple, maroon, white and near-black.

▲ **PINKROOT**

Spigelia marilandica, Zones 5 to 9

Hummers will be especially grateful when you add pinkroot to your garden. A rugged and handsome wildflower of modest size—from 1 to 2 feet tall and wide—it blooms from late spring to early summer. The spiky tube-shaped flowers are bright pink and yellow.

◄ **RED-HOT POKER**

Kniphofia spp., Zones 4 to 9

Terrific in mixed flower borders or small groupings, torchlike red-hot poker plants grow up to 4 feet high and deliver bright plumes of orange, red, yellow, white and green. For best results, well-draining soil is important; the roots will rot in boggy conditions. Nectaring birds and swallowtails love it.

▲ **ROCK CRESS**

Arabis caucasica, Zones 4 to 8

Add some springtime fragrance to your garden with this delicate bloomer. Rock cress prefers dry soil and full sun. Give this short-and-sweet ground cover a haircut after it's finished blooming to help it fill out and look tidier for the rest of the growing season.

▲ **SEDUM**

Sedum spp., Zones 3 to 10

Many cultivars of this late-season favorite boast bold hued foliage, ranging from red to purple to gold. Other types of this versatile succulent, including the popular Autumn Joy, have broccoli-shaped light-green flower heads that slowly change to pink and deepen to burgundy; later, the seeds nourish songbirds. Most sedums are hardy in all but the harshest climates.

SHOWY MILKWEED
Asclepias speciosa, Zones 3 to 9

🦋 | ☀️

This 3- to 6-foot-tall butterfly magnet and monarch host boasts rose-colored flowers of 3 to 5 inches, along with silvery foliage. In the wild, it's found in Western and Central North America, growing along sandy and rocky shores and in prairies. Showy milkweed thrives in moist, well-draining soil (including rock-filled sites), but also tolerates more arid conditions.

◀ **STOKES' ASTER**
Stokesia laevis, Zones 5 to 9

🦋 | ☀️

Colorful fringed petals fan out from the center of this native daisy that's beloved by butterflies. Each amply sized bloom ranges from 3 to 5 inches wide, creating an impressive display in a flower bed border. Regular deadheading will extend the bloom time, sometimes even into fall.

STRAWBERRY
Fragaria spp., Zones 2 to 11

This sweet treat will bring lots of fliers to your yard. Plants have various growing habits, so choose the one that's right for you. Just remember that you won't be able to harvest the fruit until the second growing season. The wait will be worth it!

SWAMP MILKWEED
Asclepias incarnata, Zones 3 to 9

A fragrant nectar and host plant, swamp milkweed is a top performer in moist soil. Less pushy than common milkweed, this 3- to 5-foot native blooms in white or pink.

11 Milkweed Picks for Bees & Butterflies

Green milkweed
Heartleaf milkweed
Poke milkweed
Prairie milkweed
Purple milkweed
Sand milkweed
Spider milkweed
Tall green milkweed
Wavy-leaved milkweed
Whorled milkweed
Woollypod milkweed

▲ **SWEET WILLIAM**

Dianthus barbatus, Zones 3 to 9

A biennial beauty, sweet William tends to grow to about 2 feet tall, but dwarf varieties are easy to come by, as well. Each flower-packed stem makes a complete bouquet!

◄ **TULIP**

Tulipa, Zones 4 to 8

Few flowers announce the arrival of a season the way the tulip does. Available in many sizes, blooming rates and colors, the tulip is the most popular bulb in the world. Why the narrow hardiness area? Most require a long winter to bloom. In warmer areas, you can force tulip bulbs by chilling them in the fridge for eight to 10 weeks before planting.

▲ TURTLEHEAD
Chelone spp., Zones 3 to 9

Bring life to partly shady areas with this distinctive fall butterfly magnet. Pink, purple or white flowers bloom on spikes that grow from 16 to 40 inches high. This native plant thrives in moist soil, so it's an ideal addition to a bog garden.

▶ VERONICA
Veronica spp., Zones 3 to 9

Ever-popular veronica has a wide range of growing habits, and blooms in cool shades. It thrives in well-draining, fertile soil and full sun, but will likely tolerate a little bit of part shade.

VIOLET
Viola, Zones 3 to 10

Try this pretty option if you've got partial shade. Perennial violets bloom in spring and prefer partial shade. Annual violas actually prefer full sun but will thrive in cooler temperatures of partial shade. They're dainty plants with a maximum height of only about 6 inches.

▲ VIRGINIA BLUEBELLS
Mertensia virginica, Zones 3 to 8

With its sprays of nodding, dainty, bell-shaped flowers, this perennial adds sophistication to any garden. Plant this 1- to 2- foot charmer alongside summertime bloomers whose foliage will cover the spent wildflower. Despite its name, you'll also find Virginia bluebells in pink and white.

▶ WINTER HEATH
Erica carnea, Zones 5 to 7

Through most of the winter and into early spring, this reliable, low-growing plant puts on an attractive show of small urn-shaped purple-pink flowers. Songbirds like the cover, and early-arriving butterflies stop by for nectar. Plant it in acidic soil.

▶ YARROW
Achillea spp., Zones 3 to 9

This easygoing, long-lasting perennial ranges from 6 inches to nearly 5 feet high. Yarrow comes in a rainbow of colors and is suited to most growing conditions.

Trumpet Vine

CHAPTER FOUR
Grasses & Vines

Blue fescue grass

Blue oat grass

BLUE FESCUE GRASS
Festuca glauca, Zones 4 to 8

Lovers of this grass don't mind having the blues at all. You'll warm up to blue fescue, too, for its compact, container-friendly tufts and bright hue. It grows to about 6 to 12 inches tall.

BLUE OAT GRASS
Helictotrichon sempervirens, Zones 4 to 8

Planted in a border or container, or used as a stand-alone accent, blue oat grass makes a big statement. This ornamental attains greater height and stronger blades than blue fescue while showing off a similarly striking shade of blue. For best foliage color, give it full sun in cool regions and light shade in warm areas.

◄ BOSTON IVY
Parthenocissus tricuspidata, Zones 4 to 8

In autumn, this quick-growing vine is bedecked with scarlet, trident-shaped foliage and midnight-blue berries that attract birds. It thrives in sun or shade and looks stunning when covering a wooden fence. (It can destroy brickwork.) Vines climb to 50 feet.

CANARY CREEPER

Tropaeolum peregrinum
Annual, Perennial
in Zones 9 to 10

Take a close look at the bright
yellow flowers and you'll see
the inspiration for the common
name. Grow this climbing
nasturtium in full sun to part
shade with moist, well-drained
soil. Train it on a trellis, grow it
in a hanging basket or allow it to
scramble through other plants.

▲ **CANDY CORN PLANT**
Manettia luteorubra,
Annual, Perennial in Zones 10 to 11

This noncaloric candy corn is fun for gardeners of all ages. The orange tubular flowers are tipped in yellow, making them look like the Halloween treat. Grow it in light shade and moist, well-drained soil.

◄ **CLEMATIS**
Clematis spp., Zones 4 to 9

By September, many clematis varieties are petering out, but other species, such as golden (*C. tangutica*) and sweet autumn clematis (*C. terniflora*), are at their peak. Either way, clematis is a fall wildlife winner, because once the petals fall, birds seek out the spindly seed clusters.

CUP AND SAUCER VINE

Cobaea scandens, Annual, Perennial in Zones 9 to 11

🐦 | ☀️

A vigorous grower, give this vine a sturdy support to climb and display its cup-shaped, aromatic flowers. The blooms open green and then mature to purple, lasting about four days. Grow in full sun and provide a bit of afternoon shade in hotter regions.

▲ FEATHER REED GRASS
Calamagrostis x *acutiflora*
Zones 4 to 9

This plant's tall, sweeping, upright habit gives it textural winter eye appeal, while the birds enjoy the seeds. In fact, this drought-tolerant grass is handsome almost year-round. Starting in summer, its green foliage is topped by plush silvery-bronze to purple flowers that persist into snowy weather.

▶ FIGWORT
Asarina scandens, Annual, Perennial in Zones 9 to 10

Brighten the summer and fall garden with the indigo, violet, pink or white flowers of figwort. Grow it in full sun to part shade on a trellis or allow the stems to spill over the edge of a hanging basket.

▲ FOUNTAIN GRASS
Pennisetum alopecuroides, Zones 5 to 9

With full tufts of fuzzy, drooping flower spikes that turn into natural birdseed, this ethereal grass seems to be heaven-sent. One or more of its many varieties will add charm to your backyard wildlife habitat. Fountain grass reaches 2 to 5 feet.

▼ GOLDEN SEDGE
Carex elata, Zones 5 to 9

This plant's fine, arching green and yellow leaves seem to glow in sunny spots. The 2- to 3-foot-tall evergreen tufts make a bold statement all year long.

◀ GRAPE
Vitis spp., Zones 2 to 9

This high-sugar fruit provides lots of energy for birds, and a number of sphinx moths use it as a host plant. The woody, deciduous vines grow up to 30 feet long, do best in full sun and produce late-summer and autumn fruit in a variety of sizes and flavors; some are unpalatable to humans.

▼ HYACINTH BEAN VINE
Dolichos lablab, Annual, Perennial in Zones 10 to 11

This purple beauty will quickly cover a trellis or fence and its green leaves, white, pink or purple-pink flowers and purple pods provide season-long color. Grow hyacinth bean in full sun to partial shade. Despite being an annual, it will often reseed in the garden.

▲ LICORICE VINE
Helichrysum petiolare, Annual

🦋 | ☀️

Licorice plant's fuzzy, silvery foliage grows long enough to trail, readily weaving throughout surrounding plants. This vine thrives in partial shade to full sun and spreads out to 6 feet.

▶ MANDEVILLA
Mandevilla, Annual, Perennial in Zones 10 to 11

🐦 🐝 | ⛅ ☀️

A drought-tolerant vine that can be grown in a container, hanging basket or right in the garden, mandevilla thrives in full sun to part shade and well-drained soil. You'll find many new cultivars with white, pink, maroon, crimson and bicolor flowers.

BACKYARD TIP
If you live in a colder climate, you can overwinter your mandevilla. Just bring it indoors and place it in a warm, sunny location.

9 Native Grasses for Birds

Big bluestem
Andropogon gerardii

Blue grama grass
Bouteloua gracilis

Indian rice grass
Achnatherum hymenoides

Little bluestem
Schizachyrium scoparium

Muhly grass
Muhlenbergia spp.

Northern sea oats
Chasmanthium latifolium

Prairie dropseed
Sporobolus heterolepsis

Sideoats grama
Bouteloua curtipendula

Switchgrass
Panicum virgatum

▲ **MISCANTHUS**
Miscanthus sinensis, Zones 4 to 9

 |

You'll be on cloud nine with the fluffy frosted tops of this ornamental grass. The big, showy flower heads and height of up to 12 feet give it a profile that's both dramatic and graceful. In fall, some plants' silky gray panicles turn maroon or purplish-brown—all last through winter. Plant miscanthus in a sun-drenched area.

▲ **MORNING GLORY**
Ipomoea spp., Annual

 |

The flowers on this popular vine open to greet the day. Plants climb up to 12 feet high. Cultivars Grandpa Ott and Heavenly Blue are surefire choices.

▲ PASSIONFLOWER

Passiflora spp., Zones 5 to 9

This quirky flower doesn't just look cool, it's a big draw for Southern wildlife. Nectar-seekers visit blossoms, while certain types of longwings and other butterflies use the vine as a host. The fragrant flowers come in shades of purple, blue, red, pink, yellow and white, and make way for berries that birds devour. Vines range in length from 15 to 50 feet—most gardeners let the tendrils climb walls and fences, while others use it as a groundcover.

▶ SCARLET RUNNER BEAN

Phaseolus coccineus, Annual

Grow scarlet runner bean, a hummingbird favorite, in a sunny spot in your vegetable or flower garden. You can grow these long vines on a trellis, arbor or fence. Regular harvesting will keep the plant producing more pods and its scarlet flowers blossoming.

▲ SWITCHGRASS
Panicum virgatum, Zones 4 to 9

This fuss-free and versatile ornamental is a smart pick for wet or dry conditions or partial shade, as long as it's planted in well-draining soil. Growing narrow and upright with a pouf of seed heads in fall, switchgrass can reach more than 5 feet tall. Birds take advantage of the thick growing habit and use it for winter cover, and satyrs and skippers use it as a host.

◄ TRUMPET HONEYSUCKLE
Lonicera sempervirens, Zones 4 to 9

Plant this and you won't be the only one to fall for its elegant blossoms—Hummingbirds are suckers for trumpet honeysuckle, too. Vines with red, orange and yellow blossoms climb up to 20 feet and thrive in full sun to partial shade. Once the blooms fade, finches, thrushes and other songbirds will stop by to nibble the berries. This North American native is also host to the spring azure and the snowberry clearwing moth.

TRUMPET VINE
Campsis radicans
Zones 4 to 9

  |

There's a reason you see so many photos of hummingbirds at trumpet vines. They love this sweet beauty! A perennial classic, trumpet vine grows up to 40 feet, easily filling a trellis with its orange-red or yellow blooms. The trumpet vine sphinx moth uses it as a host plant. Unwanted suckers will generally be discouraged if cut off.

◀ VIRGINIA CREEPER
Parthenocissus quinquefolia, Zones 3 to 9

The deep blue berries on this vigorous grower are an important food source for migrating birds in fall, when Virginia creeper is most gorgeous. The vines grow in sun or shade and can reach 50 feet in length. Keep an eye out for resident Pandora sphinx moths.

Monarch on
butterfly bush

CHAPTER FIVE
Trees & Shrubs

◀ ABELIA
Abelia spp., Zones 5 to 11

When abelia's sweet, trumpet-shaped flowers open, you'll know that spring is in full swing. Cue the hummingbirds and butterflies! Varieties of this long-blooming shrub reach between 5 and 15 feet tall, growing best in a sunny spot protected from the wind.

AMERICAN BITTERSWEET
Celastrus scandens, Zones 3 to 8

Bittersweet's showy orange berries are a favorite of more than a dozen bird species. Growing up to 30 feet tall, it offers ample shelter. Choose it over its invasive cousin, Oriental bittersweet (*C. orbiculatus*).

▼ ARTEMISIA
Artemisia spp., Zones 3 to 8

Reliable artemisia is valued for its beautiful, slender gray to silver leaves on tall, arching stems or in low mounds, which range from 1 to 5 feet high and wide. These plants are tough and trouble-free.

American bittersweet

AUTUMN SAGE
Salvia greggii, Zones 6 to 10

Catch migrating hummingbirds with reddish shades of salvia. The annual of this plant (*S. splendens*) has always been a good choice for those flying jewels, so now try adding the perennial version to your garden. Grow this 2- to 3-foot-tall native Texan shrub in a sunny spot in well-drained soil. Want another color? Autumn sage is also available in orange, purple, white and more.

▲ BARBERRY

Berberis spp., Zones 3 to 8

This thorny shrub is grown for its abundant foliage in spring, summer and fall and will provide much-needed shelter for birds in cold weather. For the best color and fruit, grow your barberry in full sun. Try it as a hedge. Barberry will attract bluebirds, gray catbirds, northern mockingbirds, brown thrashers and others. Before planting, check to see if it's invasive in your area.

◀ BEAUTYBERRY

Callicarpa spp., Zones 5 to 8

For a berry bush that's a little unusual, try beautyberry. Its spring or summer flowers are alluring to butterflies, and its fall fruit lasts well into winter in some regions. In others, especially the South, winter songbirds devour the bright-purple berries. This fast-growing shrub will reach about 4 feet tall.

▶ BIGLEAF MAPLE

Acer macrophyllum, Zones 5 to 7

Even if you don't believe bigger is always better, check out this tree, which boasts the largest leaves of any maple—each is up to a foot wide! A year-round winner for wildlife, bigleaf maple attracts bugs that feed migrating and local birds, produces edible seeds and flowers in spring and, at 70 feet tall and wide, offers lots of protection for nesting and roosting. It's a host for the western tiger swallowtail, too.

▲ BLACK CHOKEBERRY
Aronia melanocarpa, Zones 3 to 9

🐦 🦋 🐝 | ⛅ ☀️

A lovely and low-maintenance shrub all year, this chokeberry develops bluish-black fruit that songbirds eat in fall and winter. Butterflies like the spring flowers, and some coral hairstreaks use it as a host. Plants grow 3 to 6 feet tall and up to 10 feet wide. They thrive in full sun or part shade and moist, well-draining soil.

◀ BLUE SPIREA
Caryopteris spp., Zones 5 to 9

🦋 🐝 | ☀️

Add some cool hues to your landscape, and you'll be seeing butterflies in no time. Blue spirea's tiers of blue or purple florets make this a late-summer all-star. Most types of this shrub are about 3-1/2 feet tall and 5 feet wide and grow best in light, well-draining soil in full sun or light shade.

 **BOXWOOD**
Buxus spp., Zones 5 to 9

A top choice among landscapers for hedges and topiaries, this evergreen is covered in masses of green or variegated foliage and thrives in sites with partial shade. Because its structure is so dense, it offers ample protection to winter songbirds. Many slow-growing cultivars reach just 5 feet.

▶ **BUTTERFLY BUSH**
Buddleja davidii, Zones 5 to 9

A top nectar plant for many winged species, heat- and drought-tolerant butterfly bush grows up to 15 feet tall. The arching branches are tipped with tiny purple, white, pink or yellow blooms from midsummer through frost. It's invasive in some areas, but noninvasive species are available.

Tips for Growing Shrubs

1 Water a newly planted shrub thoroughly to help settle the soil. Add enough water to moisten the top 6 to 12 inches of soil.

2 After that, shrubs need thorough, but much less frequent watering.

3 Apply a layer of mulch around new plantings. This helps conserve moisture and moderate soil temperatues.

▲ **BUTTONBUSH**
Cephalanthus occidentalis, Zones 5 to 10

Round white flower heads with needlelike protrusions make honey-sweet buttonbush unmistakable. Shrubs are generally about 6 feet tall but occasionally far surpass that. Consistently moist soil is a must; downright wet soil, a plus.

▲ CAMELLIA
Camellia spp., Zones 6 to 11

A popular Southern evergreen, camellia flowers in the fall, winter or early spring, depending on the variety. Camellias are ideal for landscaping and produce beautiful rose-shaped blooms, usually in red, pink or white. Birds will appreciate the shrub for the shelter it provides. Expect camellia to be anywhere from 3 to 20 feet high.

◀ COLORADO BLUE SPRUCE
Picea pungens, Zones 3 to 7

Our feathered friends love the thick branches and prickly needles that offer winter shelter, whether it's from stormy weather or nearby predators. Blue spruce cones also produce seed for food. This tree does best in full sun and grows up to 60 feet tall, but dwarf cultivars are readily available, as well.

◄ **COMMON ALDER**
Alnus glutinosa, Zones 3 to 7

If your yard is plagued by wet or just plain poor soil, consider planting common alder. Migratory birds eat the bugs on the late-winter and early-spring catkins, and winter birds eat the seeds in the cones. Eventually reaching 80 feet high and 30 feet wide, the common alder also offers plenty of shelter. Before planting, ensure that it isn't invasive in your area.

▼ **COMMON BEARBERRY**
Arctostaphylos uva-ursi, Zones 2 to 6

Rocky and sandy soils are best for this hardy, low-growing evergreen ground cover, making it a good choice for drought-tolerant gardens. Bearberry, also known as kinnikinick, produces tiny white or pink flowers in spring and summer, and long-lasting bright-red berries in fall. It's also a host plant to some elfins and fritillaries.

▶ COMMON CHOKECHERRY

Prunus virginiana, Zones 2 to 7

An ideal addition to a protective thicket for both butterflies and birds, chokecherry grows 20 to 30 feet high and wide. It produces clusters of pink or white flowers in spring and red berries that deepen to purple by late summer.

▼ CORALBERRY

Symphoricarpos x *doorenbosii*, Zones 2 to 7

With berries in hues of pink and purple, this hybrid is decorative in gardens and delicious for birds. Bushes reach 6 feet tall and thrive in full sun. Prune coralberry in early spring: You'll encourage new growth and see an abundance of berries the following year.

◀ COTONEASTER
Cotoneaster spp., Zones 3 to 11

🐦 🦋 🐝 | ☀️

Whether they're deciduous, evergreen or semi-evergreen shrubs or trees, cotoneasters sport red and orange berries that songbirds love. They grow in full sun to partial shade in fertile, well-draining soil and range from 1 to 15 feet tall. In summer, you may notice butterflies sampling nectar from the white flowers.

CRABAPPLE
Malus spp., Zones 3 to 9

🐦 🐝 | ☀️

Everyone loves crabapple's lightly fragrant white, pink to rosy-red spring flowers, but consider the colorful fruit, too, when choosing one. Look for fire blight- and scab-resistant varieties to increase the beauty and reduce maintenance.

▶ CRAPE MYRTLE
Lagerstroemia indica,
Zones 7 to 9

Crape myrtle is a year-round belle in the South, where it thrives in the warmth and blooms from July to September. The spectacular flowers won't stop attracting butterflies, bees and hummingbirds. You can even remove the first wave of flowers to encourage a second bloom. Grow this heat-tolerant beauty in full sun, and it might get to be 10 feet or more.

▼ DOGWOOD
Cornus spp., Zones 2 to 8

Want a wildlife garden showstopper? Look no further. These berry-rich garden favorites feed robins, bluebirds, cardinals and dozens of other backyard birds during cold months. Butterflies and other pollinators stop by while the shrubs are flowering, while some species are hosts, as well. Dogwoods do best in full sun to partial shade, but the light requirements vary by species.

5 Dogwoods for Birds

Flowering dogwood
Cornus florida

Japanese flowering dogwood
Cornus kousa

Pacific dogwood
Cornus nuttallii

Pagoda dogwood
Cornus alternifolia

Red twigged dogwood
Cornus sericea

▲ DWARF SPRUCE
Picea, Zones 2 to 7

 |

Bring the majesty of evergreens to
your containers with dwarf spruce.
Pyramids, globes or mounds of green,
blue-green or yellow foliage create
year-round interest. Grow these in
full sun and moist, well-drained soils.
Avoid dry, hot locations.

▶ EASTERN ARBORVITAE
Thuja occidentalis, Zones 3 to 7

 |

This tree is dense, with a pyramidal
shape and clusters of small seed-
bearing cones. It has a classic conifer
look (but can be pruned to any shape
you want) and provides generous
coverage for birds. Plus, nurseries offer
plenty of cultivars to choose from. But
beware: Deer love it, too.

▶ EASTERN WHITE PINE
Pinus strobus, Zones 3 to 7

With long green needles and a quick growing habit, eastern white pine is a good choice for any yard, particularly sunny ones. It reaches 50 to 80 feet tall and 20 to 40 feet wide, so its verdant silhouette is sure to stand out in winter. The deep branches are hospitable to birds during harsh weather, and the cones are a go-to food source for nuthatches and many other seedeaters.

▼ ELDERBERRY
Sambucus spp., Zones 3 to 9

Birds and butterflies alike take shelter among elderberry's branches. The summer flowers entice swallowtails, hairstreaks and hummers, as well as other pollinators, and birds flock to the late-summer and autumn berries. Species range in height from 10 to 20 feet, and cultivars offer colorful foliage, from black to chartreuse.

◄ FALSECYPRESS
Chamaecyparis, Zones 4 to 9

Mounded, upright or spreading—take your pick among this diverse group of evergreens. The foliage texture and color, along with interesting growth habit, will make these a focal point in your container garden. Most types tolerate full sun to light or partial shade and prefer moist, well-drained soil.

FIRETHORN
Pyracantha coccinea, Zones 5 to 9

Though it has glossy green foliage for most of the year, it's the compact bunches of pea-size red, orange or yellow berries that get all the attention. The spring or summer flowers are sought after by nectaring butterflies.

▼ FLOWERING DOGWOOD
Cornus florida, Zones 5 to 8

Thanks to flowering dogwood's pink and white bracts surrounding small green flowers, butterflies and other pollinators pay frequent visits in spring. Many birds nest among the branches, and later in the growing season enjoy the bright-red berries. This lovely ornamental reaches 20 to 30 feet tall and grows best in partial to full sun.

Firethorn

FOTHERGILLA
Fothergilla spp., Zones 4 to 8

With bluish foliage that turns gold, orange and purple in fall, this shrub is a garden standout long after its fluffy spring flowers—attractive to warblers and vireos that eat resident insects—fade. Larger varieties of fothergilla reach 8 feet tall, while dwarf cultivars are less than half that size. Plant it in a sunny spot with acidic soil.

◀ FRINGE TREE
Chionanthus virginicus, Zones 4 to 9

The fringe tree entices butterflies with its panicles of creamy-white flowers. This slow-growing tall shrub or tree usually starts from seed and tends to reach just 20 feet. Sphinx moths use the fringe tree as a host plant, and more than 75 species of birds are known to feast on its blue-black fruit.

▼ HAWTHORN
Crataegus spp., Zones 3 to 9

Commonly used as a border tree in backyard landscapes, hawthorn is a wildlife haven that feeds nectar-seeking butterflies in spring and hungry songbirds in fall. Species of this tree thrive in full sun and grow from 20 to 45 feet tall. All hawthorns have appealing burgundy to orange fall color.

▶ HEMLOCK
Tsuga spp., Zones 4 to 8

Hemlock trees are shade-tolerant—especially when they're young—and make good hedges. This tree will tolerate sun if it's sheltered and the soil conditions are good. One variety in particular, Cole's Prostrate Canada hemlock (*T. canadensis*), shown here, has a weeping silhouette with a low, spreading habit and cascading branches. It provides dense shelter for ground-feeding birds such as towhees and juncos.

▼ HIBISCUS
Hibiscus spp., Zones 5 to 11

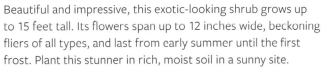

Beautiful and impressive, this exotic-looking shrub grows up to 15 feet tall. Its flowers span up to 12 inches wide, beckoning fliers of all types, and last from early summer until the first frost. Plant this stunner in rich, moist soil in a sunny site.

▲ HYDRANGEA
Hydrangea, Zones 3 to 10

Gardeners have relied on hydrangeas for years to provide showy summer color. Easy to care for, they happily flower even in partial shade. Bigleaf hydrangeas (*Hydrangea macrophylla*) are ideal for mild climates but usually won't flower in regions with cold winters. In those areas, try cultivars of sevenbark hydrangea (*Hydrangea arborescens*), which typically produce big white blooms.

◄ JUNIPER
Juniperus spp., Zones 2 to 9

Also known as redcedar, this tree can grow up to 50 feet tall. A juniper will serve as a secure roosting and nesting site. Some birds, including waxwings, enjoy the berry-like cones, as well. Plant juniper in fall so its roots have time to become established before winter.

LILAC
Syringa spp., Zones 3 to 8

🐦 🦋 🐝 | ☀

Among spring's most anticipated sights and scents, the lilac attracts butterflies and hummingbirds and serves as a nesting site for songbirds. A deciduous shrub growing up to about 20 feet tall and wide, this sun lover is at its best in small groups or as a specimen plant.

◄ LINDEN
Tilia spp., Zones 2 to 9

Growing in full sun, some linden types can reach 100 feet tall, offering plenty of shelter for local fliers. In mid-June to early July, the cone-shaped tree produces fragrant white to pale-yellow blooms that invite a host of pollinators, especially bees; later, the flowers yield small nutlike fruit that feeds foraging birds when the weather cools down. Linden's heart-shaped, light-green leaves turn a soft butternut-yellow in autumn.

▼ MADRONE
Arbutus menziesii, Zones 7 to 11

You may know this broadleaf evergreen for its elegant form and reddish-brown bark, but the waxwings know madrone for the berries. Madrone's berry clusters may include red, orange and yellow fruit at the same time. The dark green leaves make a striking backdrop to the white flowers. Plant it in a mixed border or mulch bed to minimize leaf and blossom cleanup. It prefers warm, dry locations.

◀ MAHONIA
Mahonia spp., Zones 5 to 11

This evergreen shrub has spiny-edged leaves that often resemble those of holly, and bears clusters of blue-black berries. Various species grow from 1 to 12 feet in light shade. This shrub's yellow flowers emerge early, providing nectar for overwintering hummingbirds and butterflies.

MOCKORANGE
Philadelphus spp., Zones 3 to 11

Butterflies love this shrub's scented white spring flowers, and so will you. Varieties range in size from just 18 inches to more than 10 feet tall. Most types of mockorange prefer full sun and thrive in well-draining soil.

▶ MOUNTAIN ASH
Sorbus spp., Zones 2 to 7

A smart landscaping pick for compact backyards, this medium-size ornamental tree boasts spectacular yellow and red fall foliage. The red or orange berry clusters attract flocks of cedar waxwings, robins, gray catbirds, eastern bluebirds, thrashers and at least a dozen other species. Mountain ash is also a great host plant for eastern tiger swallowtails.

▼ NEW JERSEY TEA
Ceanothus americanus, Zones 3 to 8

A low-growing shrub 3 feet high and 5 feet wide, New Jersey tea supplies ample shelter and nectar for visiting fliers. It's also a host to some azure and duskywing butterflies. Sweet-smelling, 2-inch panicles of small white flowers begin blooming in late spring.

◀ OAK
Quercus spp., Zones 3 to 10

Young white oaks are a favorite for hairstreak and skipper caterpillars. Plant one that's native in your area.

▼ PIERIS
Pieris, Zones 4 to 7

Start spring off with fragrant white flowers both you and the early pollinators will love. Then stand back and admire the show as the new growth emerges red. Evergreen pieris grows well in full sun or partial shade; afternoon shade is best where summers are hot.

PINKSHELL AZALEA
Rhododendron vaseyi, Zones 4 to 7

Brighten a partly shady woodland garden with the sweet blossoms of pinkshell azalea. This spring- and summer-blooming shrub attracts nectar-seeking fliers. Plant in a spot with plenty of room, since it can reach up to 15 feet tall. Despite the name, some varieties also bloom in white.

▲ POTENTILLA
Potentilla fruticosa, Zones 2 to 7

When many other flowering shrubs' show is all but a memory, potentilla, or bush cinquefoil, is just beginning its long blooming season. The pink, yellow, red or white blossoms of this drought-tolerant plant will last until the first hard frost, attracting migrating butterflies. Its dense branches provide protection for birds year-round. This compact shrub is about 3 feet high and up to 5 feet wide.

◄ PUSSY WILLOW
Salix discolor, Zones 4 to 8

In midspring, velvety silver-gray catkins emerge from the bare stems of this small upright tree. Migrating birds stop by to eat little insects on the branches, which play host to a number of butterflies once the blue-green leaves appear. Some backyard birds, like cardinals and finches, eat the flower buds as well. Plant pussy willow in moist, well-draining soil in a sunny place where it has room to expand.

BACKYARD TIP

Any species of buckeye will add charm to your landscape. The leaves are very distinctive and the showy red flowers attract hummingbirds.

▲ **RED BUCKEYE**

Aesculus pavia, Zones 4 to 8

In late spring, the red buckeye unfurls 6-inch-long upright panicles of tubular red flowers. It grows to just 15 feet tall and 10 feet wide, so one of these would look right at home in most backyards. Moist, well-draining soil and partial shade are the ideal growing conditions for this compact tree.

◀ **REDBUD**

Cercis spp., Zones 4 to 9

An early-spring showstopper, this tree bursts with a profusion of purple, red, pink or white blossoms before the leaves emerge. Redbud's blooms attract hummers, butterflies (especially hairstreaks) and other pollinators. The seeds appeal to chickadees, goldfinches and others, and nuthatches and woodpeckers eat the insects on the bark. Henry's elfin caterpillars use redbuds as a host. Plant yours where there's plenty of space, as they're often wider than they are tall.

ROSE OF SHARON
Hibiscus syriacus, Zones 5 to 9

When other flowers are spent, this late bloomer becomes a generous source of energy for hummingbirds. A member of the hibiscus family, it bears charming trumpet-shaped flowers that bloom from late summer through midautumn. In optimal conditions, including moist, well-draining soil and lots of sunshine, rose of Sharon can climb to 10 feet or more.

GARDENING FOR BIRDS, BUTTERFLIES & BEES

◀ RUGOSA ROSE
Rosa rugosa, Zones 2 to 8

Love roses but hate the hassle? This fast-growing species flourishes virtually anywhere and reaches up to 8 feet tall. Rugosa roses handle poor soil conditions, from sandy to salty, and produce bright red rose hips that attract countless birds. Pollinators visit during the growing season.

▶ SASSAFRAS
Sassafras albidum, Zones 4 to 9

Your yard will be a hit with fliers when you plant a sassafras tree. It's a host for some swallowtails, and more than a dozen species of birds (especially thrushes) enjoy the female plants' fruit. This aromatic tree reaches 80 feet and thrives in moist, acidic soil in a mostly sunny spot. Transplanting can be tough, so avoid jostling the sapling's taproot when transferring to the ground. Pull out volunteers that sprout from seed to discourage a colony from forming.

▶ SERVICEBERRY
Amelanchier spp., Zones 2 to 9

Looking for a birds-and-blooms bonanza for your yard? Try serviceberry. These small trees or shrubs, which thrive in sun or part shade, provide many months of interest, with butterfly-friendly spring flowers, summer berries that songbirds enjoy, plus colorful fall foliage.

DID YOU KNOW?
It won't take long for birds to clear a tree of its berries. Sometimes they're gone in just a few weeks.

◀ SPICE BUSH
Lindera benzoin, Zones 4 to 9

The namesake of spicebush swallowtails, spice bush is also a host plant for the related eastern tiger butterfly. In spring, aromatic star-shaped green-yellow flowers appear, followed by red berries (on female plants) that are prized by songbirds. This woodland shrub grows up to 10 feet tall and wide and is an ideal candidate for a partly sunny spot that needs some interest, especially in autumn.

▼ SUMAC
Rhus spp., Zones 2 to 9

Masses of brilliantly hued leaflets and bunches of bristly berries set sumac apart in the fall. Spring flowers beckon to butterflies; later, bluebirds, robins, flickers and others enjoy the fruit. These shrubs (which can range in height from 8 inches to 20 feet tall) are vigorous spreaders, so be sure you pick a site with plenty of room.

SUMMERSWEET
Clethra alnifolia, Zones 3 to 9

Native to the Eastern U.S., fragrant summersweet is a pretty addition to any site. Spikes bearing bell-shaped pink or white blooms emerge in late summer, just in time to entice southbound fliers. Summersweet reaches 8 feet tall; for a smaller space, try Hummingbird—it's 2 to 3 feet tall.

TULIP TREE
Liriodendron tulipifera, Zones 5 to 9

Though hard to see from afar, the tulip tree's spring to early-summer flowers will dress up your yard. The cup-shaped blooms have light-yellow petals with orange bases. Grosbeaks, finches and others eat the seeds. Be patient: Most types won't begin to flower for 10 to 12 years. But you won't have to wait for wildlife: Birds favor the tree for nesting, and it's a host for eastern tiger swallowtail caterpillars. This columnar tree can reach up to 100 feet tall.

Weigela

▲ VIBURNUM
Viburnum spp., Zones 2 to 9

Among the most popular of ornamental shrubs and small trees, members of this genus are sought after for three reasons: They're beautiful, versatile and easy to grow. What's more, the flowers, the foliage and the colorful fruits all contribute to viburnums' year-round beauty. Ample moisture is the only requirement to keep in mind.

WEIGELA
Weigela spp., Zones 3 to 9

In addition to its pretty, trumpet-shaped late-spring flowers, which entice returning hummingbirds, weigela boasts attractive foliage throughout the growing season. In some varieties, leaves change color in fall. Sizes range from 2 to 8 feet tall and wide.

▶ WILD BLACK CHERRY
Prunus serotina, Zones 3 to 9

Popular among caterpillars—such as blues, hairstreaks and admirals—that munch on its leaf and flower buds, the wild black cherry's fruit is also sought after by birds later in the year. This fast-growing tree shines in fall, when its leaves turn yellow or red. It prefers some sun and is salt- and drought-tolerant.

▲ WINTERBERRY
Ilex verticillata, Zones 3 to 9

🐦 🦋 🐝 | ⛅ ☀️

Few deciduous shrubs garner as much cold-weather interest as winterberry. Unlike most of its holly cousins, it drops its leaves in the autumn, so nothing detracts from the brilliance of the red berries. You'll love the colorful fruit, and the birds will love you for it. In warmer weather, watch for Henry's elfins: This is a host plant for these little butterflies.

▶ WISTERIA
Wisteria floribunda, Zones 5 to 9

🐦 🦋 🐝 | ☀️

There's nothing quite like a blooming garland of wisteria to add romance to a spring backyard—especially when the butterflies (including skippers, sulfurs and blues) and hummingbirds arrive. Provide ample support for the vine's heavy, woody limbs, which can extend to more than 30 feet, and prune wisteria each year after it flowers.

BACKYARD TIP
Wisteria has a lovely scent, but it is an aggressive grower. It needs to be cut back annually with pruning in order to keep it in check.

◀ WITCH HAZEL
Hamamelis x *intermedia,* Zones 5 to 9

Just when you're convinced that winter will never end, witch hazel explodes with masses of fragrant ribbon-petal flowers in copper, yellow or red. Depending on the cultivar and location, this deciduous shrub may blossom as early as January and hold onto its blooms until March. Later on, birds forage for the fallen seeds. The gray-green leaves turn yellow-orange with frost.

YUCCA
Yucca filamentosa, Zones 4 to 11

There's a good reason that so many gardeners (especially those in the Southwest) use yucca as a backyard centerpiece. It's about as drought-tolerant as they come. Spiky evergreen leaves create a mound that's so substantial that birds nest within it, while hummingbirds crave the nectar the beautiful columnar white flowers provide. Types of this shrub can reach 3 to 12 feet tall when in bloom.

Northern cardinal

CHAPTER SIX
Backyard Bird Profiles

Bird Range
Map Key

■ winter
■ summer
■ year-round
■ migration

Eastern bluebird

Bluebirds

Many, many years ago, the return of bluebirds—especially eastern bluebirds—to northern states in March signaled the arrival of warmer weather. But with mild winters becoming more common, many bluebirds now spend winters in their nesting areas all across the North.

A week or two after the male arrives, the female appears. Then, to the accompaniment of his own incessant warbling, the male pursues his chosen mate from one perch to another, often showing her spots available for nesting.

MAKING A COMEBACK

In the early to mid-1900s, bluebirds almost became extinct. But today, all three species—eastern, western and mountain—are at healthy population levels, and the future looks bright.

They still face challenges, however, such as competition for nesting sites from house sparrows, house wrens, European starlings and tree swallows. Often, just about the time a pair of bluebirds begins to nest, one of the four enemy birds takes over.

House wrens will even poke holes in the bluebirds' eggs. What's especially frustrating about this aggressive behavior is that once they win the battle, these other birds often vacate the house.

Nesting starts early among bluebirds, so they can raise at least two broods each year. It's common for the first brood to help their parents feed the second brood, a practice known as "cooperative breeding." As the song says, these lovely and popular birds are truly the "bluebird of happiness," bringing excitement, color and adventure to any backyard.

EASTERN, WESTERN AND MOUNTAIN BLUEBIRD

Sialia sialis, S. mexicana and *S. currucoides*, respectively.

Length: 7 inches.

Wingspan: 13 to 14 inches.

Distinctive Markings: Males generally have a blue back, wings and head, with a white belly, except for the mountain bluebird, which is brilliant blue all over. Orange on the breast extends onto the throat. Females generally have the same markings, but duller, except for western females, which are gray overall with pale-blue feathers on tail and wings.

Voice: Soft *tru-al-ly, tru-al-ly* warble for eastern; mountain is similar but higher pitched; and western's is a subdued *f-few, f-few, f-few.*

Habitat: Backyards and farmland.

Nesting: Built mostly by the female, the nest is made of dried grasses and lined with finer grasses, hair and feathers. She lays four to six pale-blue eggs between March and July for eastern, April and May for western and April and July for mountain.

Diet: Insects and berries.

Backyard Favorite: Live mealworms.

Western bluebird

Mountain bluebird

DID YOU KNOW?
Cold-loving pine grosbeaks can be found in parts of North America, Europe and Asia. True to its name, this songbird is attracted to pinecones.

▲ **PINE GROSBEAK**
Pinicola enucleator
Length: 9 inches.
Wingspan: 14 inches.
Distinctive Markings: The males are red with gray. Females are grayish with yellow on their heads.
Voice: A short, clear and musical warble.
Habitat: Open areas and edges of coniferous forests, along streams or ponds and in wooded suburbs.
Nesting: Bulky, loose nest of twigs and roots. Female lays three to five blue-green speckled eggs.
Diet: Tree seeds, berries and some insects.
Backyard Favorite: Sunflower seeds.

◄ **EVENING GROSBEAK**
Coccothraustes vespertinus
Length: 8 inches.
Wingspan: 14 inches.
Distinctive Markings: Males are yellow and brownish with a black tail, white wing patches and a yellow band above their eyes. Females are grayish with similar marks.
Voice: Sharp, high and trilling *kleerr* call.
Habitat: Coniferous forests and western mountains.
Nesting: Shallow cup-shaped nests. Lays two to five blue or turquoise eggs.
Diet: Insects in summer; seeds and buds in winter.
Backyard Favorite: Sunflower seeds at a tray feeder.

▲ BLACK-HEADED GROSBEAK

Pheucticus melanocephalus

Length: 8-1/4 inches.

Wingspan: 12-1/2 inches.

Distinctive Markings: Males have black head, brownish-orange underparts and bicolored bill; black and white tail and white wing patches. Female is brown with stripes.

Voice: Whistled warble, faster, higher and choppier than the rose-breasted.

Habitat: Along water and open woods.

Nesting: Build in dense outer foliage of tree or shrub.

Diet: Seeds, berries and insects.

Backyard Favorites: Sunflower and safflower seeds.

▲ ROSE-BREASTED GROSBEAK

Pheucticus ludovicianus

Length: 8 inches.

Wingspan: 12-1/2 inches.

Distinctive Markings: Male is black and white with a rose-red triangle on his breast. Females are dark brown with white streaked underparts.

Voice: Long, continuous robinlike whistle.

Habitat: Small trees and shrubs in gardens and parks.

Nesting: Males and females build loose nests.

Diet: Forages in trees for seeds, insects and fruit.

Backyard Favorites: May come to feeders for sunflower and safflower seeds.

▲ AMERICAN ROBIN
Turdus migratorius
Length: 10 inches.
Wingspan: 17 inches.
Distinctive Markings: Male has orange breast, black head and tail, white around eyes and on throat. Females are duller.
Voice: Loud, liquid song: *cheerily, cheer-up, cheerio.*
Habitat: Yards, fields, farms and woods.
Nesting: Three to four pastel-blue eggs in a neat, deep cup made of mud and grass.
Diet: Earthworms. Also eats insects, berries and some seeds.
Backyard Favorites: Fruit, sunflower seeds and peanut butter.

◄ WOOD THRUSH
Hylocichla mustelina
Length: 7-3/4 inches.
Wingspan: 13 inches.
Distinctive Markings: Potbellied bird with a reddish crown and neck, white eye ring and a bold black-spotted breast.
Voice: Tranquil, peaceful liquid song: *ger-al-deeeeen.*
Habitat: Wooded areas.
Nesting: Females build nest in the crotch of a tree or shrub. Resembles a robin's nest.
Diet: Insects and a wide range of fruits and berries.
Backyard Favorites: Feeders with fruit or bird cakes made with cornmeal, peanut butter and beef suet.

▲ NORTHERN MOCKINGBIRD

Mimus polyglottos

Length: 10 inches.

Wingspan: 14 inches.

Distinctive Markings: Both sexes are gray with grayish-white undersides and white patches on the bottom of their wings.

Voice: Almost unlimited variations. Talented mimic. Repeats songs several times with a pause before a new series.

Habitat: Backyards, pastures, hedges and woodland edges.

Nesting: Pairs build cup-shaped nests in the fork of a shrub. Lays three to six blue or green eggs with brown splotches.

Diet: Insects, fruit and berries.

Backyard Favorites: Berries, suet and mealworms.

▶ MOURNING DOVE

Zenaida macroura

Length: 12 inches.

Wingspan: 18 inches.

Distinctive Markings: Both are brown-gray and pigeon-like with a long, pointed tail with white edges conspicuous in flight.

Voice: Coo-ah, cooo, cooo, coo.

Habitat: Open woods, evergreen plantations, orchards, farmlands and suburban backyards and gardens.

Nesting: Commonly found in an evergreen. Builds a loose, bulky platform of sticks in which it lays two pure-white eggs. Pairs raise two to five broods each year.

Diet: Seeds and plant materials.

Backyard Favorites: Seed mix or cracked corn.

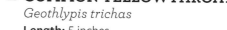

▲ **COMMON YELLOWTHROAT**

Geothlypis trichas

Length: 5 inches.

Wingspan: 6-3/4 inches.

Distinctive Markings: Male has a bright yellow throat and black mask across its forehead. Females lack the mask.

Voice: A gentle whistle of *wichity-wichity-wichity*.

Habitat: Prairie, pine forest and wetlands.

Nesting: Bulky nest filled with dead grasses, hair and more.

Diet: Mostly insects, including grubs and caterpillars.

Backyard Favorite: Birdbaths.

◀ **YELLOW WARBLER**

Dendroica petechia

Length: 5 inches.

Wingspan: 8 inches.

Distinctive Markings: Male is bright yellow with reddish-brown streaks on breast; female is duller yellow.

Voice: *Sweet sweet sweet sweet sweeter sweeter* or *sweet-sweet-sweet-chit-tit-tit-teweet*.

Habitat: Gardens, marshes, orchards and thickets.

Nesting: Strong, compact cup of firmly interwoven hemp, grasses and plant down. Built in upright fork of shrub or tree.

Diet: Insects—mostly caterpillars.

Backyard Favorite: Birdbaths, especially with moving water.

► YELLOW-RUMPED WARBLER
Dendroica coronata

Length: 5-1/2 inches.

Wingspan: 9-1/4 inches.

Distinctive Markings: Grayish males have a yellow crown. Females are brownish. Both have bright-yellow patches on their rump and flanks, best seen in flight.

Voice: High-pitched *swee swee swee swee swee*.

Habitat: Woodlands, mountains, scrub and open areas.

Nesting: A neat, deep cup on a horizontal conifer branch.

Diet: Insects in summer, and berries in winter.

Backyard Favorites: During nesting season, birdbaths. In winter, they will eat bird cakes.

▼ PROTHONOTARY WARBLER
Protonotaria citrea

Length: 5-1/2 inches.

Wingspan: 8-1/2 inches.

Distinctive Markings: A bright-golden warbler with blue-gray wings and tail, with white below. Female is duller.

Voice: A series of loud, ringing sweet notes.

Habitat: Swamps, bottomlands and near water.

Nesting: Females construct nests in cavities out of mosses, rootlets, twigs and leaves; four to six creamy, spotted eggs.

Diet: Mostly aquatic insects, plus some mollusks.

Backyard Favorite: Birdbaths.

◀ **EASTERN AND WESTERN SCREECH-OWL**
Otus asio and *O. kennicottii*
Length: 8-1/2 inches.
Wingspan: 20 inches.
Distinctive Markings: Gray, red or brown with heavy streaks below and darker bars on back; small ear-like tufts on head. The western's bill is slightly darker.
Voice: A tremulous cry or whinny.
Habitat: Deciduous trees and near waterways.
Nesting: In a natural cavity or large birdhouse, the female lays four to five white eggs.
Diet: Insects, mammals, birds, fish, spiders and reptiles.
Backyard Favorite: A large birdhouse in which to roost and nest.

▼ **GREAT HORNED OWL**
Bubo virginianus
Length: 18 to 25 inches.
Wingspan: 3 to 5 feet.
Distinctive Markings: Large ear tufts; regional coloring.
Voice: *Whoo! Whoo-whoo-whoo! Whoo! Whoo!* Female call is higher pitched.
Habitat: Wooded areas, including parklands in suburban and urban sites.
Nesting: Hollow trunks where female lays one to three eggs in late winter. Also inhabits man-made platforms.
Diet: Primarily mice, rats and rabbits, but also small mammals, birds, insects, reptiles and amphibians.
Backyard Favorites: Large trees for roosting and hollow or broken trunks for nesting.

▲ HORNED LARK
Eremophila alpestris
Length: 7-1/4 inches.
Wingspan: 12 inches.
Distinctive Markings: Males have a black mask and breast band surrounded by bright yellow. Females look duller. Two horned tufts of feathers point backward.
Voice: Song is a few lisping chips, followed by a rapid, tinkling and rising trill.
Habitat: Large, open grasslands in rural areas.
Nesting: On the ground, the female builds a shallow cup of course stems, leaves and grasses. Females incubate the three to five eggs.
Diet: Seeds and insects, usually in open fields.
Backyard Favorite: Uncommon at feeders, but they may eat seeds on the ground when food is scarce.

▶ EASTERN AND WESTERN MEADOWLARK
Sturnella magna and *S. neglecta*
Length: 9-1/2 inches.
Wingspan: 14 to 14-1/2 inches.
Distinctive Markings: Species appear identical: a black "V" from their throats to their bright-yellow breasts.
Voice: The western song starts with several whistles, followed by a jumble of sounds. The eastern's song is a simple, clear and slurred: *spring o' the year.*
Habitat: Prairie-like areas.
Nesting: Three to five spotted white eggs on the ground.
Diet: Mostly insects, some grains.
Backyard Favorite: Large, unmowed lawns.

DID YOU KNOW?
The western meadowlark is the official bird of six U.S. states: Kansas, Nebraska, Montana, Oregon, North Dakota and Wyoming.

RUBY-THROATED HUMMINGBIRD
Archilochus colubris

Length: 3-3/4 inches.

Wingspan: 4-1/2 inches.

Distinctive Markings: Ruby-red throat on male; both sexes have metallic-green back and head.

Voice: Faint; a rapid series of chipping notes.

Habitat: Areas with plentiful nectar-rich flowers.

Nesting: Cup-shaped nest the diameter of a quarter and camouflages it with lichens. Lays two tiny, white eggs.

Diet: Nectar, insects and tree sap.

Backyard Favorites: Sugar water and bright, trumpet-shaped flowers.

▶ BLACK-CHINNED HUMMINGBIRD

Archilochus alexandri

Length: 3-3/4 inches.

Wingspan: 4-3/4 inches.

Distinctive Markings: Male has a black chin with a purple band below it. Female's throat is pale.

Voice: A high, weak warble.

Habitat: Mountainous areas from foothills to summits, gardens and areas near rivers.

Nesting: A round cup made of plant down, about 1-1/2 inches across and coated with spiders' silk, usually attached to a branch or tree fork. Females lay two white eggs.

Diet: Flower nectar, tree sap, pollen and insects.

Backyard Favorite: Sugar water.

▶ RUFOUS HUMMINGBIRD

Selasphorus rufus

Length: 3-3/4 inches.

Wingspan: 4-1/2 inches.

Distinctive Markings: Male is reddish brown on back, head and tail; scarlet throat. Female is metallic green above, with pale, rust colored sides.

Voice: Call note is *chewp chewp*.

Habitat: Open areas and woodland edges.

Nesting: May nest in loose colonies, with up to 10 nests.

Diet: Nectar and tree sap.

Backyard Favorites: Attracted to red flowers; sugar water at feeders.

▶ ANNA'S HUMMINGBIRD

Calypte anna

Length: 4 inches.

Wingspan: 5-1/4 inches.

Distinctive Markings: Adult males have iridescent red crown and throat. Females have red patch on throat and white markings over eyes.

Voice: Call is a high sharp *stit*.

Habitat: Gardens and parks that provide nectar-producing flowers.

Nesting: Made of plant down held together with spider webs. Females lay two small white eggs.

Diet: Nectar, sugar water, spiders, small insects and tree sap.

Backyard Favorite: Sugar water.

▲ TREE SWALLOW
Tachycineta bicolor
Length: 5-3/4 inches.
Wingspan: 14-1/2 inches.
Distinctive Markings: Iridescent greenish-blue above and white below. Females may be slightly duller.
Voice: Early morning singers while in flight. Also uses quick, repetitious call of *silip* or *chi-veet*.
Habitat: Open fields and woodland edges near water.
Nesting: Female builds nest of grasses and white feathers in tree cavities and bluebird boxes.
Diet: Insects, plus berries and seeds in cold weather.
Backyard Favorite: Offer white feathers for nesting material.

PURPLE MARTIN
Progne subis
Length: 7 to 8 inches.
Wingspan: 16 to 17 inches.
Distinctive Markings: Males are iridescent blue-black all over, while females and juveniles have light-gray breasts.
Voice: Low, rich and liquid gurgling.
Habitat: Near water and large open areas.
Nesting: Eastern birds primarily choose man-made housing. Western birds often nest in natural tree and cactus cavities.
Diet: Flying insects.
Backyard Favorite: Will eat crushed eggshells for calcium.

Purple martin

▶ **CHIMNEY SWIFT**
Chaetura pelagica
Length: 5-1/4 inches.
Wingspan: 14 inches.
Distinctive Markings: Both males and females are sooty gray, with short bodies and long curved wings.
Voice: Constant chattering during flight.
Habitat: Open—often urban—areas.
Nesting: Using sticks and thick glue-like saliva, they affix nests to walls. Females usually lay four to five white eggs.
Diet: Flying insects.
Backyard Favorite: Faux chimneys attract them to nest.

▶ **WHIP-POOR-WILL**
Caprimulgus vociferus
Length: 9 inches.
Wingspan: 18 inches.
Distinctive Markings: Heavily mottled with gray, black and brown above and paler below. The male has white patch borders below its black throat and the tips of its outer tail feathers. Females are buff-colored in those areas.
Voice: Distinctive repeated night call: *whip-poor-will*.
Habitat: Open deciduous woodlands.
Nesting: None. The female lays two light-brown spotted eggs in dead leaves on the ground.
Diet: Small flying insects caught in flight.
Backyard Favorite: Bugs.

◄ **HOUSE WREN**
Troglodytes aedon
Length: 4-3/4 inches.
Wingspan: 6 inches.
Distinctive Markings: Dark-brown above and lighter below.
Voice: The male's bubbling, chattering, repetitive song rises and then falls at the end.
Habitat: Along the edges of woodlands and yards with trees.
Nesting: Will nest in strange places—boots, car radiators and mailboxes—as well as in small birdhouses. Nest built of sticks and lined with plant fibers, feathers and rubbish.
Diet: Insects, including caterpillars.
Backyard Favorite: A small birdhouse near a tree.

▼ **CAROLINA WREN**
Thryothorus ludovicianus
Length: 5-1/2 inches.
Wingspan: 7-1/2 inches.
Distinctive Markings: Rusty-brown with a white eye stripe.
Voice: Loud, piercing song often heard as *tea-kettle, tea-kettle, tea-kettle*.
Habitat: Brush and heavy undergrowth in forests, parks, wooded suburbs and gardens.
Nesting: Builds bulky nest of grass, bark, weed stalks, feathers and other materials in tree cavities, woodpiles, sheds, flower baskets, mailboxes and more. Female incubates five to six pale-pink spotted eggs.
Diet: Spiders and insects, plus some berries and seeds.
Backyard Favorites: Peanuts, suet and peanut butter.

▲ WHITE-BREASTED NUTHATCH

Sitta carolinensis

Length: 5-3/4 inches.

Wingspan: 11 inches.

Distinctive Markings: Males and females look similar, with a blue-gray back and wings, black cap and white breast.

Voice: Nasal *yank-yank-yank* call.

Habitat: Areas with plentiful trees.

Nesting: Builds in natural cavities and birdhouses. Lays five to 10 white eggs with multicolored markings.

Diet: Insects and larvae; tree nuts, seeds and berries.

Backyard Favorites: Sunflower seeds, unsalted peanuts, birdseed mix and suet.

▶ RED-BREASTED NUTHATCH

Sitta canadensis

Length: 4-1/2 inches.

Wingspan: 8 1/2 inches.

Distinctive Markings: Black eye line with a white stripe directly above it, rust-colored breast; female similar.

Voice: High-pitched nasal *yenk, yenk, yenk.*

Habitat: Evergreen forests, and wooded yards and parks.

Nesting: Hole or cavity in a tree or a nestbox.

Diet: Insects, berries, nuts and seeds.

Backyard Favorites: Sunflower seeds and suet.

BACKYARD TIP

Nuthatches love trees, and they're not likely to be found far away from them. If you're going to plant, consider native oaks, maples, hickories, pines or spruces.

NORTHERN CARDINAL
Cardinalis cardinalis

Length: 8-3/4 inches.

Wingspan: 12 inches.

Distinctive Markings: Male is bright red with a black face. Also has a prominent crest and red bill. Female is fawn colored with red accents.

Voice: Over two dozen different songs. The most common song is: *What cheer! What cheer! What cheer!*

Habitat: Sheltered backyards, woodland edges and parks.

Nesting: Three to four whitish-gray eggs with brown speckles. Builds a nest of twigs and grasses hidden in dense trees or shrubs.

Diet: Seeds in winter; insects, such as beetles and cicadas, in the summer; berries and other fruits when they are available.

Backyard Favorites: Sunflower seeds, safflower seeds and cracked corn.

BACKYARD TIP
Attract spotted towhees to your backyard with brushy, shrubby or overgrown borders. They also might feed on any seed that has fallen below feeders.

▲ EASTERN TOWHEE

Pipilo erythrophthalmus

Length: 8-1/2 inches.

Wingspan: 10-1/2 inches.

Distinctive Markings: Black head, back and tail with a white belly, orange-red sides and red or white eyes, varies by region.

Voice: Musical with a slow song: *Drink your teeeeee.*

Habitat: Pastures, woodland edges and brushy yards.

Nesting: Builds nest near the ground. Female lays three to four gray speckled eggs.

Diet: Insects, spiders, caterpillars, seeds, berries and small salamanders.

Backyard Favorites: Oats or flaxseed scattered on the ground; suet.

▲ SPOTTED TOWHEE

Pipilo maculatus

Length: 8-1/2 inches.

Wingspan: 10-1/2 inches.

Distinctive Markings: Black head, back and tail with a white belly, orange-red sides and white wing marks.

Voice: Wide variety of songs, usually high-pitched introductory notes followed by a trill. Also has a buzzy, rapid trill.

Habitat: Pastures, woodland edges and brushy yards.

Nesting: Builds nest near or on the ground. Female lays three to four speckled gray eggs.

Diet: Insects, spiders, caterpillars, seeds, berries and small salamanders.

Backyard Favorites: Oats or flaxseed scattered on the ground; suet.

▲ HAIRY WOODPECKER

Picoides villosus

Length: 9-1/4 inches.

Wingspan: 15 inches.

Distinctive Markings: Black-and-white checked back, with long, heavy bill and inconspicuous tuft. Females similar to males, but lack red mark on back of head.

Voice: Strong *peek* or *peech*.

Habitat: Deciduous forests.

Nesting: Pair excavates cavity. Females usually lay four white eggs.

Diet: Insects, larvae of woodborers, fruit and nuts.

Backyard Favorites: Suet, sunflower seeds, meat scraps and peanut butter.

▲ RED-HEADED WOODPECKER

Melanerpes erythrocephalus

Length: 9-1/4 inches.

Wingspan: 17 inches.

Distinctive Markings: Red feathers completely cover head and neck. Male and female look the same.

Voice: Harsh *queeah, queeah, queeah*.

Habitat: Open woodlands.

Nesting: Excavates hole in trees, posts or utility poles.

Diet: Insects, berries and nuts.

Backyard Favorites: Cracked sunflower seeds and suet.

◄ RED-BELLIED WOODPECKER

Melanerpes carolinus

Length: 9-1/4 inches.

Wingspan: 16 inches.

Distinctive Markings: Males have a zebra-striped back, red hood and nape with a reddish tinge on bellies. Females are identical, except for red napes.

Voice: Males and females drum on trees and siding to "sing." They also have a call note that sounds like *chiv, chiv, chiv.*

Habitat: Bottomland woods, swamps, coniferous and deciduous forests, and shade trees in backyards.

Nesting: Both sexes drill a nesting cavity in a tree, utility pole or wooden building. The female lays four or five pure-white eggs, which both parents incubate.

Diet: Larvae, insects, acorns and berries.

Backyard Favorites: Medium cracked sunflower seeds on a tray feeder, suet, orange halves and sugar water.

◄ DOWNY WOODPECKER

Picoides pubescens

Length: 6-3/4 inches.

Wingspan: 12 inches.

Distinctive Markings: White belly and black-and-white elsewhere; male has a small red spot on the back of its head. Resembles a small hairy woodpecker.

Voice: Both male and female "sing" in early spring by drumming on trees. Their call note is a single *tchick.*

Habitat: Open deciduous woodlands.

Nesting: Pair creates a cavity in a tree. The female lays four or five pure-white eggs.

Diet: Mostly insects, but also fruit, seeds and nuts.

Backyard Favorites: Suet, bird cakes, cracked sunflower and safflower seeds.

◄ PILEATED WOODPECKER
Dryocopus pileatus
Length: 16-1/2 inches.
Wingspan: 29 inches.
Distinctive Markings: Both sexes have a bright-red crest, but the male's extends down its forehead. The male has a red streak at the base of its bill; the female's is black.
Voice: Both sexes have a *yucka-yucka-yucka* call.
Habitat: Woodlands, swamps and wooded backyards.
Nesting: Pairs excavate cavities in trees, often near water, for nesting. Females lay three or four white eggs on a bed of wood chips.
Diet: Insects, nuts, fruits and seeds.
Backyard Favorites: Suet on a mounted feeder; nuts.

▼ NORTHERN FLICKER
Colaptes auratus
Length: 12-1/2 inches.
Wingspan: 20 inches.
Distinctive Markings: Eastern and western males sport black and red mustaches, respectively. Females don't have the mustache. For eastern birds, the wings and tail include yellow feathers; these are red in western birds.
Voice: *Flicka, flicka* or loud *wick, wick, klee.*
Habitat: Backyards, orchards and open woodlands.
Nesting: Males and females excavate nesting cavities in dead trees, utility poles and fence posts. Females lay six to eight white eggs, and males incubate them at night.
Diet: Insects, fruits, berries and weed seeds.
Backyard Favorite: Large birdhouse at least 10 feet above the ground.

▲ PINE SISKIN
Carduelis pinus
Length: 5 inches.
Wingspan: 9 inches.
Distinctive Markings: Sexes appear similar, with brown-streaked bodies and touches of yellow on wings and tails. Males have more yellow plumage, visible during flight.
Voice: Ranges from a tuneful *sweeet* to a harsh *zzzzz*.
Habitat: Backyards and coniferous forests.
Nesting: Females build shallow nests of twigs and grasses, lined with fur or feathers.
Diet: Seeds, nuts, vegetable shoots, rock salt and insects.
Backyard Favorites: Nyjer in a tube feeder with multiple perches. Also will eat cracked sunflower seeds.

▶ TUFTED TITMOUSE
Baeolophus bicolor
Length: 6-1/2 inches.
Wingspan: 9-3/4 inches.
Distinctive Markings: Gray above and white below, rusty-brown flanks, prominent pointed crest and large dark eyes
Voice: Call sounds like *peto, peto, peto.*
Habitat: Deciduous woodlands, preferably in swamps and river bottoms; residential wooded areas.
Nesting: Natural cavities in trees.
Diet: Insects, berries and seeds.
Backyard Favorites: Sunflower and safflower seeds, nuts, peanut butter and suet.

▲ DARK-EYED JUNCO

Junco hyemalis

Length: 6-1/4 inches.

Wingspan: 9-1/4 inches.

Distinctive Markings: Common characteristics are dark eyes, white-edged tails and dark hoods; juncos interbreed freely.

Voice: Trills vary, from dry notes to tingling sounds.

Habitat: Near feeders, forests and bogs.

Nesting: Cup-shaped nest on ground. Lays four to six eggs.

Diet: Seeds, nuts and grains in winter; insects, berries and grass seeds in summer.

Backyard Favorites: Birdseed and cracked corn on ground.

◄ COMMON REDPOLL

Carduelis flammea

Length: 5-1/4 inches.

Wingspan: 9 inches.

Distinctive Markings: Brown-streaked feathers with red crown; adult males have rose-colored feathers on their upper breast.

Voice: Short, repeated notes. Mainly call notes and trills.

Habitat: Scrub forests, tundra, brushy pastures and thickets.

Nesting: Constructed with twigs, lined with grass, moss, feathers, rootlets and animal fur.

Diet: Tree seeds as well as grass and weed seeds; insects.

Backyard Favorites: Nyjer, millet and sunflower seeds.

▶ EASTERN PHOEBE

Sayornis phoebe

Length: 7 inches.
Wingspan: 10-1/2 inches.
Distinctive Markings: Dark olive on top; slightly darker head.
Voice: Birds call their own name, repeating *fee-bee, fee-bee.*
Habitat: Woodlands and forest edges.
Nesting: Shelflike projection over windows, on rafters or on bridge girders. They build a nest of weeds, grasses, plant fibers and mud. Females incubate four to five white eggs.
Diet: Almost entirely insects, usually caught in flight.
Backyard Favorite: Berries.

BLACK-CAPPED CHICKADEE

Poecile atricapilla

Length: 5-1/4 inches.
Wingspan: 8 inches.
Distinctive Markings: Black cap and chin, white cheeks, gray back.
Voice: *Chick a-dee-dee-dee* is its call, which many will recognize. Its song is a *phoe-bee* tune.
Habitat: Woodlands, thickets, parks and wooded backyards.
Nesting: Six to eight white eggs with brown spots. Uses birdhouses and natural cavities to protect its nest made of plant fibers, wool, hair and moss.
Diet: Insects, berries and seeds.
Backyard Favorites: Sunflower seeds, suet and nyjer.

BACKYARD TIP
It's super easy to attract orioles to your backyard in early spring. Put out grape jelly and orange halves. With any luck, they'll stick around all summer!

Orioles

Few songbirds are more visually striking—or create more excitement for birders—than orioles.

No matter where you live in the continental United States and parts of southern Canada, you should be able to attract a brilliant oriole to your backyard. All you have to do is know what they crave (oranges and grape jelly fit the bill)—and offer some tree cover for their protection.

True, orioles have a sweet tooth. But it seems their desire for citrus wanes a bit around the time they start feeding their youngsters insects and caterpillars at the nest. That's when it's important to have a sugar-water feeder.

COLORFUL FOR BLACKBIRDS

Even though they're one of the most brilliant backyard birds, all North American orioles belong to the blackbird family. Unlike other members, however, they spend most of their time high up in the treetops, rather than on the ground.

When orioles return to their northern breeding territories, they look for tree cover and stay well hidden in their search for food. The females also build their incredible nests high above the ground, weaving them from fibers of grasses, grapevines and milkweed.

FAB FIVE

Nine different orioles live throughout the continental United States during the breeding months, but the most common are the Baltimore, Bullock's, orchard, hooded and Scott's. Four others—the altimera, Audubon's, spot-breasted and streak-backed—are rarely spotted or occupy very small territories along the southernmost borders of the United States.

But no matter what the species is, if you cover the basics—trees, fruit and sugar water—there's a good chance a flashy oriole will visit your backyard in spring.

BALTIMORE, BULLOCK'S AND ORCHARD ORIOLE

Icterus galbuba, I. bullockii and *I. spurious,* respectively.
Length: 7-1/4 to 9 inches.
Wingspan: 9-1/2 to 12 inches.
Distinctive Markings: Male Baltimore has full black hood, Bullock's has black crown with orange cheeks and white wing patches and orchard has black hood and chestnut feathers. The female Baltimore is drab yellow with dusky brown wings, the Bullock's is mostly yellow with gray back and the orchard is dusky yellow-green and gray.
Voice: Short series of clear whistles in a varied pattern for Baltimore, short series of nasal-like whistles for Bullock's and high, lively warble for orchard.
Habitat: Deciduous woodlands, open areas and suburbs.
Nesting: Pouch-like structure woven from plant fibers.
Diet: Beetles, bugs, caterpillars and fruit.
Backyard Favorites: Fruit slices, fruit trees or shrubs and nectar feeders.

Bullock's oriole

Orchard oriole

▲ SONG SPARROW
Melospiza melodia
Length: 6-1/4 inches.
Wingspan: 8-1/4 inches.
Distinctive Markings: Streaked with brown; side streaks join to form central breast spot. Grayish stripe over each eye.
Voice: Male song begins with *sweet, sweet, sweet* followed by shorter notes and a trill. Distinctive call note is *chimp*.
Habitat: Low, open, weedy or brushy areas.
Nesting: Well-hidden ground or low nest. Female lays three to five eggs that are greenish-white and heavily splotched.
Diet: Small weed and grass seeds in fall and winter; insects.
Backyard Favorites: Birdbaths and ground-level tray feeders with seeds, each surrounded by thickets or brush.

◄ WHITE-THROATED SPARROW
Zonotrichia albicollis
Length: 6-3/4 inches.
Wingspan: 9 inches.
Distinctive Markings: White throat, yellow patches in front of eyes and heads striped with black and white or tan.
Voice: *Old Sam Peabody, Peabody, Peabody* or *Oh, sweet Canada, Canada, Canada.*
Habitat: Gardens, woodlands and clearings.
Nesting: Builds nest from fine materials on or near the ground; three to six blue to green speckled eggs.
Diet: Weed seeds, fruits, buds and insects.
Backyard Favorites: Millet, sunflower, corn and other seeds.

AMERICAN TREE SPARROW
Spizella arborea

Length: 6-3/4 inches.

Wingspan: 9-1/2 inches.

Distinctive Markings: Brick-red cap, white stripes above the eyes, brown striped back and a black dot in the center.

Voice: A sweet canary-like trill in spring in preparation for migration; winter call is a *teelwit* note.

Habitat: Fields, backyards, open woodland and marshes.

Nesting: On the ground in remote areas, they build a nest of grasses and stems lined with feathers.

Diet: Mostly weed seeds.

Backyard Favorite: Seed mix in a feeder on or near the ground.

CHIPPING SPARROW
Spizella passerina

Length: 5 to 6 inches.

Wingspan: 8 inches.

Distinctive Markings: Rust cap, a white line above the eye and a black stripe through the eye.

Voice: A long, mechanical trill.

Habitat: Backyards, gardens and forest openings.

Nesting: Nest is loosely woven; commonly in evergreen tree.

Diet: Forages for small seeds and insects.

Backyard Favorite: Small seeds.

◄ AMERICAN GOLDFINCH
Carduelis tristis
Length: 4-1/2 to 5-1/2 inches.
Wingspan: 9 inches.
Distinctive Markings: In spring and summer, males are bright yellow with black wings, tail and forehead. Females are a duller yellow with white wing bars. In winter, both sexes are olive brown with wing bars.
Voice: Melodic flight call, *per-chick-o-ree, per-chick-o-ree*. Courtship song is a canary-like sweet song.
Habitat: Open areas such as yards, fields and groves.
Nesting: Cup-shaped nest with up to six pale-blue eggs.
Diet: Seeds and berries.
Backyard Favorite: Supply nyjer in a tube feeder with multiple ports, or in a nylon stocking.

◄ PURPLE FINCH
Carpodacus purpureus
Length: 6 inches.
Wingspan: 10 inches.
Distinctive Markings: Male has a raspberry tinge, brightest on head and rump. Tail is notched. The females and juveniles are brown-gray striped.
Voice: A *fridi ferdi frididifri fridi frr* call.
Habitat: Swamps, along streams and hillsides.
Nesting: Prefers trees in dense foliage. Female lays four to five speckled pale green-blue eggs.
Diet: Mostly a seedeater, but also feeds on weeds, grasses, berries, beetles and caterpillars.
Backyard Favorites: Sunflower seeds and millet.

◄ GRAY CATBIRD
Dumetella carolinensis
Length: 8-1/2 inches.
Wingspan: 11 inches.
Distinctive Markings: Slate-gray body with a black cap and tail and a patch of rust-red feathers under tail.
Voice: Alarm call sounds like a catlike mewing; song is a mix of notes, may mimic other songbirds.
Habitat: Dense thickets, woodland edges, overgrown fields and hedgerows.
Nesting: Builds nests in backyard shrubs or thickets near creeks or swamps. Females usually lay four glossy dark greenish-blue eggs.
Diet: Insects and berries.
Backyard Favorite: Grape jelly.

HOUSE FINCH
Carpodacus mexicanus

Length: 6 inches.

Wingspan: 9-1/2 inches.

Distinctive Markings: Males have reddish foreheads, breasts and rumps. Females and juveniles are streaked grayish brown. All have brown-streaked bellies.

Voice: A varied warble, often ending in a long *veeerrr*.

Habitat: Any wooded area or backyard.

Nesting: Low in shrubs, door wreaths or hanging baskets; lays four to five spotted bluish-white eggs.

Diet: Seeds of berries and weeds.

Backyard Favorites: Nyjer, sunflower, mixed birdseed, peanuts, fruit, suet and sugar water.

▲ WESTERN SCRUB-JAY

Aphelocoma californica

Length: 11-1/2 inches.

Wingspan: 15-1/2 inches.

Distinctive Markings: Bright blue with a white belly and gray patch on back. Sexes look alike.

Voice: Hoarse rising call of *shreeeenk* or a rapid series *quay-quay-quay* or *cheek-cheek-cheek*.

Habitat: Dense shrubbery in wooded parks and backyards.

Nesting: Bulky nest of twigs in a low tree or shrub.

Diet: Nuts, fruits, insects and small animals.

Backyard Favorites: Peanuts, suet, sunflower seeds and cracked corn.

▶ BLUE JAY

Cyanocitta cristata

Length: 11 inches.

Wingspan: 16 inches.

Distinctive Markings: Blue feathers and crest with a gray breast.

Voice: Harsh scream: *jaaay, jaaay, jaaay.*

Habitat: Backyards, parks and woodlands.

Nesting: Well hidden and often found in the crotch of a tree 10 to 25 feet above the ground. False nest of twigs built before actual nest; four to five brown-spotted greenish eggs.

Diet: Nuts, seeds, fruits, insects and frogs.

Backyard Favorites: Suet, sunflower seeds and peanuts.

▲ STELLER'S JAY

Cyanocitta stelleri

Length: 11 1/2 inches.

Wingspan: 19 inches.

Distinctive Markings: Crest and front part of body are a sooty black. The rest of body is cobalt blue or purplish.

Voice: A harsh *shaaaaar* or rapid *shek shek shek shek*.

Habitat: Evergreen forests, open areas and mountains.

Nesting: Bulky nest of large sticks held together with mud. Usually built in the fork of an evergreen.

Diet: Forages for acorns, pine seeds, fruit, insects, frogs and young of smaller birds.

Backyard Favorites: Sunflower seed and peanuts.

▶ RED-WINGED BLACKBIRD

Agelaius phoeniceus

Length: 8-3/4 inches.

Wingspan: 13 inches.

Distinctive Markings: Males have glossy black bodies with red and yellow shoulder patches. Females have brown backs and heavily streaked undersides.

Voice: *Kong-la-ree* or *o-ka-lee*.

Habitat: Fields, marshes and near water.

Nesting: Well-camouflaged grass nest among shrubs, cattails or grasses; three to five blue-green eggs with dark scrawls.

Diet: Grains, wild seeds, insects and berries.

Backyard Favorite: Birdseed mixes.

▲ **WESTERN TANAGER**
Piranga ludoviciana
Length: 7-1/4 inches.
Wingspan: 11-1/2 inches.
Distinctive Markings: Male has bright-yellow body, black wings with prominent white bars. Head turns red in spring and summer. Female is yellow with gray back.
Voice: Similar to a robin: *Queer-it, queer. Queer-it, queer.*
Habitat: Mature forests.
Nesting: Builds loose nest of twigs high in the trees. Three to five bluish-green spotted eggs.
Diet: Insects and fruit.
Backyard Favorites: Dried fruit, oranges and sugar water.

▶ SCARLET TANAGER

Piranga olivacea

Length: 7 inches.

Wingspan: 11-1/2 inches.

Distinctive Markings: Males are warm red with black wings until fall, molting to yellow-green over winter. Females look identical to yellow-green males, but with black wings and tails.

Voice: Five phrases in a rapid pattern.

Habitat: In treetops in forests, parks and residential areas.

Nesting: Shallow, saucer-shaped nests.

Diet: Insects.

Backyard Favorites: Oranges, sugar water and grape jelly.

▶ INDIGO BUNTING

Passerina cyanea

Length: 5-1/2 inches.

Wingspan: 8 inches.

Distinctive Markings: Males are completely blue during breeding season. Females are plain brown with buff-colored streaks and a hint of blue in their wing feathers.

Voice: Rapid notes, *sweet-sweet, zee-zee, seer-seer, sip-sip*.

Habitat: Overgrown fields, orchards, roadsides and thickets.

Nesting: Cup-shaped nests hidden 2 to 12 feet off the ground in weeds or shrubs. Lays three or four bluish white eggs.

Diet: Seeds, insects, grains and berries.

Backyard Favorites: Nyjer; birdbaths.

▶ LAZULI BUNTING

Passerina amoena

Length: 5-1/2 inches.

Wingspan: 8-3/4 inches.

Distinctive Markings: Male's breeding plumage is a bright-blue head, back and tail, cinnamon chest feathers and a white belly. Tan streaks appear in winter. Females are a buff color.

Voice: A bright, rapid song that descends and then rises.

Habitat: Brush or trees near open areas.

Nesting: A cup of coarsely woven grasses in a low shrub. Female lays four pale-blue eggs.

Diet: Insects and grass seeds.

Backyard Favorites: Mixed seed or hulled sunflower.

CEDAR WAXWING
Bombycilla cedrorum
Length: 7-1/4 inches.
Wingspan: 12 inches.
Distinctive Markings: Head crest, black eye mask, red tips on wings, yellow at end of tail and pale yellow belly. Sexes look alike.
Voice: Irregular rhythm of high *sreee* notes.
Habitat: Backyards, parks and open woodlands.
Nesting: Nests late in the season, so young can feed on emerging berries. Female lays four to five pale-gray spotted eggs.
Diet: Fruit, tree sap, flower petals and insects.
Backyard Favorites: Birdbaths, as well as berry-producing shrubs and trees.

▶ BOHEMIAN WAXWING
Bombycilla garrulus
Length: 6 to 8 inches.
Wingspan: 14 inches.
Distinctive Markings: Gray overall with a black mask, yellow-tipped tail, white and yellow edges on wings, and red waxlike markings on adult wings. Slightly larger than the cedar waxwing.
Voice: A mid-pitched rattling trill; lower than that of the cedar waxwing.
Habitat: Coniferous or birch forests.
Nesting: Four to six blue-gray spotted eggs in a nest lined with grasses and moss, usually high in a pine tree.
Diet: Fruit and insects.
Backyard Favorites: Prefers dried fruit or berries from a backyard feeder, or berry-producing trees.

▲ RED CROSSBILL

Loxia curvirostra

Length: 5-1/2 to 6-1/2 inches.

Wingspan: 10 to 10-3/4 inches.

Distinctive Markings: Upper and lower parts of the bill twist and overlap. Males are brick red, with dark wings and a notched black tail. Females are dusky buff yellow with dark gray wings.

Voice: Courting males sing various notes and phrases.

Habitat: Coniferous forests.

Nesting: Make saucer-like nests near tips of conifer branches. Females lay three to five brown-spotted pale-blue or pale-green eggs.

Diet: Pinecones and other tree seeds.

Backyard Favorites: Sunflower and nyjer seeds.

▲ RUBY-CROWNED KINGLET

Regulus calendula

Length: 4-1/4 inches.

Wingspan: 7-1/2 inches.

Distinctive Markings: Olive bird overall; males have a red crest, but it doesn't always show.

Voice: A whistled chant of *sii si sisisi berr berr berr pudi pudi pudi*.

Habitat: Evergreen and deciduous forests, as well as individual trees.

Nesting: A small cup-shaped nest where the female will lay 5 to 12 eggs. It is usually located high in an evergreen tree.

Diet: Insects.

Backyard Favorite: Offer water for drinking and bathing, especially during migration times.

Gulf fritillary on
chrysanthemum

CHAPTER SEVEN
Backyard Butterfly Profiles

Butterfly Range
Map Key

winter

summer

year-round

▲ MONARCH
Danaus plexippus
Wingspan: 3-1/2 to 4 inches.
Distinctive Markings: Bright orange with multiple black veins. Wings are edged in black with white speckles.
Habitat: Widespread during migration, from cities and suburban gardens to rural fields and mountain pastures. When breeding (before the southward migration), they prefer open areas with plenty of milkweed plants.
Caterpillar: White with yellow and black stripes, measuring up to 2 inches long.
Host Plant: Milkweed.

◀ QUEEN
Danaus gilippus
Wingspan: 3 to 3-3/8 inches.
Distinctive Markings: Appears similar to monarch, especially on underside of wings. Deep orangish-brown wings with black margins and thin veins. Fine white dots speckle wing edges, with larger markings on the forewings.
Habitat: Any open area where milkweed grows—meadows, fields, deserts and near waterways.
Caterpillar: Black with white bands and yellow side markings. Antennae-like filaments along back.
Host Plant: Milkweed.

▲ VICEROY
Limenitis archippus

Wingspan: 2-1/2 to 3 inches.

Distinctive Markings: Similar to the monarch with rich, russet-orange color and black veins. To set them apart, the viceroy has an extra black line curving across the hind wings.

Habitat: Canals, riversides, marshes, meadows, wood edges, roadsides, lakeshores and deltas.

Caterpillar: Mottled in color with sharply defined humps and two bristles located directly behind the head.

Host Plants: Willow, poplar, aspen, cherry, apple and hawthorn trees.

▶ MOURNING CLOAK
Nymphalis antiopa

Wingspan: 2-7/8 to 3-3/8 inches.

Distinctive Markings: Dark maroon wings with creamy-yellow bands at wing edges and bright-blue dots.

Habitat: Near water, forest edges, open woodlands, groves, parks and backyard gardens.

Caterpillar: Black with white speckles, numerous dark spines and larger red spots. The caterpillars have been known to feed in groups.

Host Plants: Elm, willow, aspen, birch and hackberry.

HACKBERRY EMPEROR
Asterocampa celtis

Wingspan: 1-3/8 to 2-1/4 inches.

Distinctive Markings: Upper sides of wings range from grayish- to reddish-brown. Wings have dark tips, distinct white dots and dark spots. Undersides of wings boast yellow-outlined dark eyespots splashed with blue.

Habitat: Wherever hackberries grow, including moist woodlands, riversides, city parks and neighborhoods.

Caterpillar: 1-1/4 inches long, green with yellow and lime stripes and dots; forked horns at both ends.

Host Plants: Hackberry trees, sugarberry, dwarf hackberry.

◄ PAINTED LADY
Vanessa cardui

Wingspan: 2 to 2-1/2 inches.

Distinctive Markings: Salmon-orange wings on top with white and black markings; five white spots on black forewing. Underside is patterned with black, brown and gray and four small submarginal eyespots.

Habitat: Virtually anywhere, particularly in open areas.

Caterpillar: Dark in color with a yellow stripe and short white or gray spines. Measures up to 1-1/4 inches long.

Host Plants: Thistle and related plants.

▲ AMERICAN LADY
Vanessa virginiensis

Wingspan: 1-3/4 to 2-5/8 inches.

Distinctive Markings: Irregular brown, yellow and orange patterns on uppersides; forewings have a black patch, a white spot below the patch and a white bar at the wing edge. Two large blue-ringed black eyespots on hind wing undersides distinguish the American lady from the painted lady, which has four small eyespots and a tiny one.

Habitat: Gardens and open areas with low vegetation, such as coastal dunes, meadows, forest edges and roadsides.

Caterpillar: Red- and white-spotted black bodies with branched black spines separated by black and green stripes.

Host Plants: Sweet everlasting, pearly everlasting, edelweiss, artemisia, ironweed and burdock.

▶ COMMON BUCKEYE
Junonia coenia

Wingspan: 2 to 2-1/2 inches.

Distinctive Markings: Brown with orange bars on forewings; large yellow-rimmed black eyespots with blue or lilac centers.

Habitat: Shorelines, roadsides, railroad embankments, swamp edges, fields and meadows.

Caterpillar: Dark green to gray with orange and yellow markings, and black spines.

Host Plants: Snapdragon, plantain, figwort, stonecrop sedums and vervain.

▶ RED ADMIRAL
Vanessa atalanta

Wingspan: 1-3/4 to 2-1/4 inches.

Distinctive Markings: Orange-red bars across center of black forewings and at base of hind wings.

Habitat: Backyards, parks, forest edges and streambeds.

Caterpillar: About 1-1/4 inches long, ranging in color from black to yellowish-green with irregular yellowish flecks and yellowish-white or black spines.

Host Plants: Mostly nettle, but also false nettle, pellitory and hops.

▼ WHITE ADMIRAL
Limentis arthemis

Wingspan: 2-1/2 to 3-5/8 inches.

Distinctive Markings: Black topwings with distinctive white bands that run across the middle on both sides.

Habitat: Areas with deciduous trees or mixed with evergreens, especially near forest edges and clearings.

Caterpillar: Mottled off-white, olive and greenish-yellow body with a bristled hump behind its head.

Host Plants: A variety of hardwood trees and shrubs, including birch, poplar, willow, black cherry and hawthorn.

▲ MILBERT'S TORTOISESHELL

Nymphalis milberti

Wingspan: 1-3/4 to 2 inches.

Distinctive Markings: Bright orange and yellow outer bands, with faint blue dots on the margins.

Habitat: Prefers higher altitudes, but can be found in all types of temperate habitats within its range.

Caterpillar: Black, spiny caterpillars have small white flecks, and a green and yellow stripe on each side.

Host Plant: Nettle.

▶ BALTIMORE CHECKERSPOT

Euphydryas phaeton

Wingspan: 1-5/8 to 2-1/2 inches.

Distinctive Markings: Black wings have orange- and cream-colored spots, plus orange crescents mark outer margins.

Habitat: Wet meadows and bogs; forest hillsides.

Caterpillar: Caterpillars are black with orange stripes and branching black spines.

Host Plants: Turtlehead, false foxglove, plantain and white ash tree.

BRONZE COPPER
Hyllolycaena hyllus

Wingspan: 1-1/4 to 1-3/8 inches.

Distinctive Markings: On males, tops of the forewings are dark copper-brown with an iridescent purple sheen. Females sport bright-orange to yellowish forewings with dark spots. Both have gray hind wings with orange edges.

Habitat: Near host plants in ditches, swamps, streams and other damp areas.

Caterpillar: Bright yellowish-green with a dark line running down the back.

Host Plants: Docks, particularly curly dock and knotweeds.

▶ MEADOW FRITILLARY
Boloria bellona

Wingspan: 1-1/4 to 1-7/8 inches.

Distinctive Markings: Reddish-orange wings with heavy black dashes and dots. This butterfly's squared-off angular forewings and its lack of silver markings distinguish it from other fritillaries.

Habitat: Moist meadows, hay fields, pastures, roadsides and bogs. Meadow fritillaries will also visit gardens.

Caterpillar: Purplish-black, sometimes mottled with yellow, with branching spines protruding from brown bumps.

Host Plant: Violet.

▶ GREAT SPANGLED FRITILLARY
Speyeria cybele

Wingspan: 2-1/8 to 3 inches.

Distinctive Markings: Orange with black-patterned markings. Yellow band and silver spots on underside of hind wings.

Habitat: Open, moist-soiled meadows, woodlands, valleys and pastures.

Caterpillar: Black with black and orange spines. Caterpillars go dormant in winter and feed on violet leaves in spring.

Host Plant: Violet.

▶ APHRODITE FRITILLARY
Speyeria aphrodite

Wingspan: 2 to 3 inches.

Distinctive Markings: Tawny-orange wings, accented with a splattering of dark spots, dashes and crescents. Underneath, the forewing is lighter with similar markings, except for a band of shiny silver spots along the edge. The hind wing sports a richer cinnamon hue and a multitude of silver spots that become more triangular away from the body.

Habitat: Wooded areas, tall-grass prairies, foothills and mountain meadows.

Caterpillar: Spiny brownish-black with black spines.

Host Plant: Violet.

▲ VARIEGATED FRITILLARY
Euptoicta claudia

Wingspan: 1-3/4 to 2-1/4 inches.

Distinctive Markings: Elongated, tawny-orange wings with dark zigzagged lines and black-dotted margins; hind wings are slightly scalloped and undersides of wings are mottled with whitish-brown patterns and splashes of orange.

Habitat: Commonly visits gardens and sunny open areas such as grasslands, fields, meadows, roadsides and mountaintops, but avoids deeply forested spaces.

Caterpillar: Salmon-red with bright-white stripes running the length of its body, rows of dark spines and knobby black horns at the head.

Host Plants: Passionflower, mayapple, flax, violets, pansies, purslane, stonecrop, moonseed and plantain.

◀ GULF FRITILLARY
Agraulis vanillae

Wingspan: 2-1/2 to 2-7/8 inches.

Distinctive Markings: The tawny undersides of the wings display a pattern of large, silvery markings.

Habitat: Gardens and sunny, open areas filled with flowers.

Caterpillar: Bright orange and covered in soft, black spines.

Host Plant: Passionflower.

▶ ANISE SWALLOWTAIL
Papilio zeliacon

Wingspan: 2-5/8 to 3 inches.

Distinctive Markings: Wide, yellow bands across wings; blue marking and orange eyespots on hind wings.

Habitat: Prefers open fields, deserts, canyons, roadways and forest clearings.

Caterpillar: Green or greenish-blue with thick, black stripes and orange dots.

Host Plants: Anise, sweet fennel, parsley, carrots, cow parsnip, citrus trees and seaside angelica.

BACKYARD TIP
If you want to start attracting butterflies with host plants, add milkweed, dill and hollyhock to your planting list. All three have incredible butterfly benefits.

▲ GIANT SWALLOWTAIL
Papilio cresphontes

Wingspan: 3-3/8 to 6-1/4 inches.

Distinctive Markings: Bright, horizontal bands of yellow dashes divide the dark topwings. Additional yellow spots line the edges. The tops also have an orange spot flanked by blue that's close to the body on each side. The tail is large with yellow centers. Undersides of wings are mostly yellow with black veining and blue and yellow spots.

Habitat: Citrus groves, sunny and open areas, forest edges, roads, rivers, glades and gardens.

Caterpillar: Brown with mottled white patches over the middle and rear. Measures almost 2-1/2 inches long at maturity. When threatened, it will produce a pair of orange horns and emit a powerful scent to ward off predators.

Host Plants: Citrus trees, prickly ash, hopwood and rue.

◄ BLACK SWALLOWTAIL
Papilio polyxenes

Wingspan: 3-1/8 to 4-1/2 inches.

Distinctive Markings: Black wings with two rows of light dots; blue markings and black-centered orange eyespots on hind wings; rows of yellow dots on abdomen.

Habitat: Open areas including gardens, fields and marshes.

Caterpillar: Bright green with black bands and yellow or orange dots.

Host Plants: Carrots, parsley, Queen Anne's lace and dill.

▶ ZEBRA SWALLOWTAIL
Eurytides marcellus

Wingspan: 2-3/8 to 3-1/2 inches.

Distinctive Markings: Triangle-shaped wings, long tails and white to greenish-blue wings with bold, black stripes. Hind wings have blue and red spots on top and a scarlet stripe on the undersides.

Habitat: Near water and in undeveloped areas such as woodlands, marshes and meadows.

Caterpillar: Young caterpillars are black with yellow and white bands. Older ones may be gray or black with yellow and white cross bands. They are larger at the front, tapering toward the rear and grow up to 1-1/2 inches long.

Host Plants: Pawpaws and related species.

▼ SPICEBUSH SWALLOWTAIL
Papilio troilus

Wingspan: 3-1/2 to 4-1/2 inches.

Distinctive Markings: Obsidian black wings. Males are greenish-blue on lower wings, females are a distinct blue on lower wings. Both have white dots along the edges and a pair of orange dots between the distinctive tails.

Habitat: Forest edges, meadows, gardens and fields.

Caterpillar: As it grows, the larva turns green and forms a set of rimmed orange eyespots on either side of the thorax.

Host Plants: Spice bush, sassafras, red bay and other bays.

GARDENING FOR BIRDS, BUTTERFLIES & BEES

◀ EASTERN TIGER SWALLOWTAIL
Papilio glaucus
Wingspan: 3-1/2 to 6-1/2 inches.
Distinctive Markings: Black tiger-like stripes on yellow background (all males and some females) and distinctive swallow-like tails. Some females are black.
Habitat: Gardens, parks, orchards and woodlands, particularly near broadleaf trees and shrubs.
Caterpillar: Dark green with enlarged front and two prominent eyespots. Overwinters in a wood-like chrysalis.
Host Plants: Ash, aspen, basswood, birch, cherry, cottonwood, sweetbay, tulip and willow trees.

◀ WESTERN TIGER SWALLOWTAIL
Papilio rutulus
Wingspan: 2-5/8 to 4 inches.
Distinctive Markings: Black tiger-like stripes on yellow background (all males and some females) and distinctive swallow-like tails.
Habitat: Gardens, parks, orchards and woodlands, particularly near broadleaf trees and shrubs.
Caterpillar: Dark green with enlarged front and two prominent eyespots. Overwinters in a wood-like chrysalis.
Host Plants: Ash, aspen, basswood, birch, cherry, sweet bay, tulip, cottonwood and willow trees.

▶ TWO-TAILED SWALLOWTAIL
Papilio multicaudata
Wingspan: 3-3/8 to 5-1/8 inches.
Distinctive Markings: One long and one medium-length twin tail on each hind wing; bright-blue patches on edges of hind wings.
Habitat: Canyons, mid-range mountains and gardens.
Caterpillar: Bright, apple-green caterpillars have a yellow hump and black-rimmed yellow eyespots. The caterpillar turns reddish-brown before it pupates.
Host Plants: Cherry, ash and common hoptree.

▶ EASTERN COMMA
Polygonia comma
Wingspan: 1-3/4 to 2-1/2 inches.
Distinctive Markings: Silver or whitish comma shape on underside of hind wing. Rusty brown upper forewings with black splotches; upper hind wings feature a broad black margin with a short tail. Sharply angled wings.
Habitat: Deciduous woodlands near water.
Caterpillar: Light green to brown and about 1 inch long, with spines on body. Overwinters in a wood-like chrysalis.
Host Plants: All members of the elm and nettle families.

When question mark butterflies are perched with their wings closed, the gray and brown colorings on their undersides help them blend in with dead leaves.

▲ SILVER-SPOTTED SKIPPER
Epargyreus clarus

Wingspan: 1-3/4 to 2-5/8 inches.

Distinctive Markings: Elongated, brownish-black wings marked with glassy yellowish-gold, squared-off spots on upper forewings, and silvery-white patches and metallic silver margins on undersides of lobed hind wings.

Habitat: Commonly visits gardens, woodlands, waterways, roadsides, parks and meadows.

Caterpillar: Growing to 2 inches long, the larvae boast light-yellow-and-green striped, spindle-shaped bodies and large, reddish-brown heads with two orange eyespots.

Host Plants: Woody legumes, including mossy locust, black locust, false indigo, hog-peanut, American potato-bean, common honeylocust and wisteria.

◄ QUESTION MARK
Polygonia interrogationis

Wingspan: 2-3/8 to 2-5/8 inches.

Distinctive Markings: Angular orange and brown-black wings with a silvery question mark on the undersides.

Habitat: Open woods, fields, parks, roadsides, orchards and sunny streamsides.

Caterpillar: Its blackish body is covered with white dots and yellow or orange lines, as well as bristle-like orange spines. The spines closest to the head are black. At maturity, it measures 1-5/8 inches.

Host Plants: Nettle, hops, hackberry and elm tree.

▲ SPRING AZURE

Celastrina ladon

Wingspan: 3/4 to 1-1/4 inches.

Distinctive Markings: The wings of adult males are a silvery violet blue from above, and grayish white with black markings and outer edges from below. Females are duller with more white and a broad black border on the topside.

Habitat: Open roadsides, clearings, forested areas and brushy fields.

Caterpillar: Colors vary from cream to yellow-green and pink to brown. They are often marked with darker patterns on the back and sides.

Host Plant: Flowering dogwood—they eat the flowers rather than the leaves because they are more nutritious.

▶ PEARL CRESCENT

Phyciodes tharos

Wingspan: 1 to 1-1/2 inches.

Distinctive Markings: Top of wings are a rich, golden orange with a patchwork of dark brown or black marks. Underneath, there is a pearl-colored crescent mark near each wing edge.

Habitat: Fields, meadows, gardens, roadsides and other open spaces.

Caterpillar: Pale brown with black head; brown branched spines and a white to yellow lateral stripe.

Host Plant: Aster.

▲ ORANGE SULPHUR
Colias eurytheme
Wingspan: 1-1/2 to 2-3/8 inches.
Distinctive Markings: There is always some orange present, whether it's the hue of the wings or splotches on the top or underside of the hind wings.
Habitat: Open spaces such as fields, prairies and yards.
Caterpillar: Small, grass-green caterpillar is covered with tiny, white hairs. White stripes edged in black run along its side. May have pink stripes below the white ones.
Host Plants: Legumes, alfalfa, clover, vetch and senna.

◄ COMMON WOOD NYMPH
Cercyonis pegala
Wingspan: 1-7/8 to 3 inches.
Distinctive Markings: Light to dark cocoa wings on top with two large eyespots amid a splash of yellow or lighter brown on both the top and bottom sides of forewing. The lower part of each wing also bears one to three eyespots on top, and up to six eyespots underneath.
Habitat: Open oak, pine and mixed woodlands, meadows, prairies, bogs, along slow rivers and streams with overhanging vegetation, thickets and grassy roadsides.
Caterpillar: Yellow-green and furry with alternating dark and light stripes running the length of its body.
Host Plants: Purpletop and other grasses.

CABBAGE WHITE
Pieris rapae

Wingspan: 1-1/2 to 2 inches.

Distinctive Markings: White forewings with dark tips. Males also bear a single black spot on each forewing, and females have two dark spots. Undersides are yellow- or gray-green.

Habitat: Gardens, fields, roadsides and areas near streams.

Caterpillar: Bright green with a thin yellow line down its back and yellow dashes on the body. It's covered in short, soft hairs that appear fuzzy.

Host Plants: Cabbage, broccoli, collards, radishes, pepper grass, nasturtiums and mustard plants.

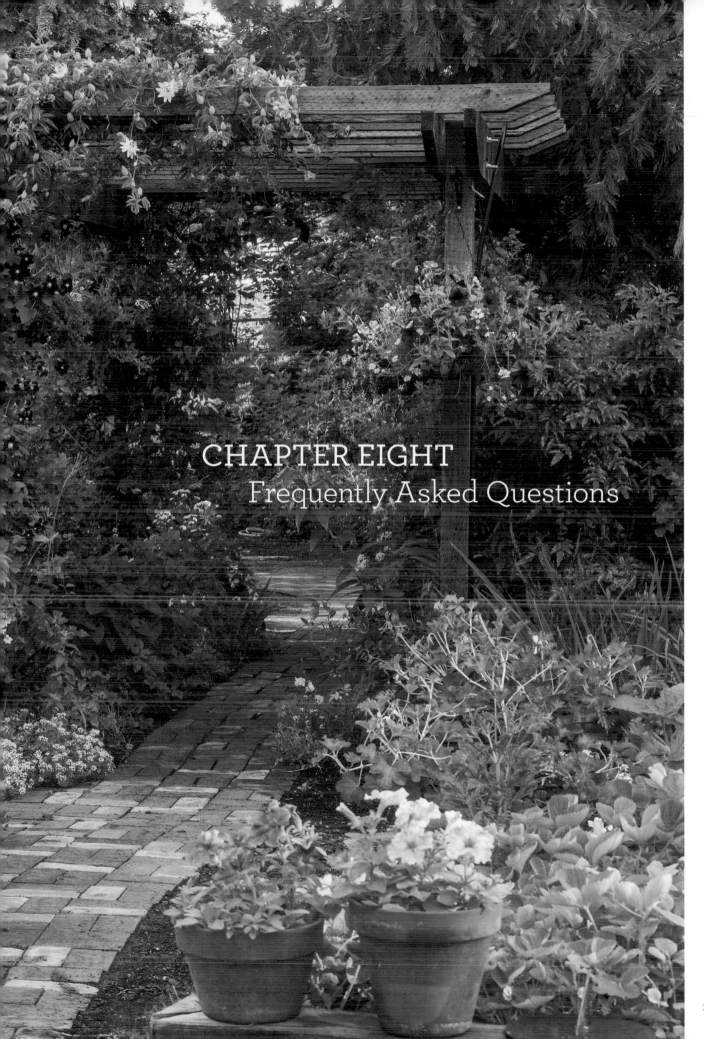

CHAPTER EIGHT
Frequently Asked Questions

Q: Are there any plants that entice fireflies?

A: Changes in gardening habits will help bring in the fireflies. Try growing the grass long. The adults lay their eggs in the soil; the larvae feed on snails, slugs and worms. Eliminate the use of chemicals to preserve their food source. Also, limit outdoor lighting that can interfere with their light signals. If there's too much light, fireflies don't glow. Include low-hanging trees and other vegetation that will provide daytime perches for these insects.

Q: How can I get hydrangeas to bloom each year?

A: Most bigleaf hydrangeas, those with pink or blue flowers, produce blooms only on the previous season's growth. In climates with cold winters, you need to protect the future flowering stems from the cold. Try encircling the plant with 4-foot-tall hardware cloth. Sink it several inches into the ground to keep out rabbits and voles, then fill with weed-free straw or evergreen boughs to insulate the plant. Wrapping the fencing with burlap or weed barrier will add another layer of insulation. Many Northern gardeners have given up on these plants and switched to the hardier panicle hydrangeas. Its flowers start out white and fade to pink before turning brown. The Endless Summer hydrangea collection is supposed to bloom on new and old growth. Moisture and proper fertilization are the keys to success.

Cityline Vienna bigleaf hydrangea

Q: How do I keep birdseed that falls to the ground from sprouting?

A: Some birdseed, such as nyjer (thistle), is sterilized and should not sprout. Other kinds, including sunflowers, are not. There is really only one safe way to keep birdseed from sprouting—present it to the birds in a tray with sides. That should prevent most spillage and solve your problem.

▲ Q: Bees love this plant! What is it?

A: This heat- and salt-tolerant perennial, *Limonium latifolium*, is known by several names, including sea lavender, wide-leaf sea lavender and statice. Hardy in Zones 3 to 9, it grows best in full sun with well-drained soil. The plant can flop and might need staking when grown in heavier clay soil. Harvest a few stems to use in dried arrangements or crafts: Cut the flower stems just before the blossoms open fully, then hang upside down in a shady, airy location to dry.

◄ Q: What type of soil is best for growing columbine?

A: Gardening success is often about patience and persistence. It seems every gardener has a plant or two that has taken several tries to succeed. Try planting columbine in full sun to partial shade with good drainage. Avoid wet, poorly drained soils, which can lead to root rot and plant death.

Q: Why do my purple coneflowers only have reddish-brown centers? There are no purple petals.

A: Aster yellows is the culprit. This disease is caused by a phytoplasma, a bacteriumlike organism that attacks more than 300 species of plants, including coreopsis, marigolds, coneflowers, carrots and potatoes, causing discolored and distorted growth.

The disease-causing organism is spread by the aster leafhopper. As this insect feeds, it transfers the disease from infected to healthy plants. Remove infected plants to prevent the disease from spreading to your healthy ones. This disease rarely kills the plant, but the phytoplasma survives in it, which can cause future infection. Fortunately, coneflowers readily reseed, and regular sanitation can help manage this disease.

Q: What are some fast-growing plants that will attract birds and other wildlife?

A: A mix of annuals, perennials, trees and shrubs will provide the food and shelter that wildlife need.

Annuals offer immediate results in any flower garden. Here are some that do well in most soil conditions: sunflower, dahlia, marigold, zinnia, verbena, nasturtium, petunia and cleome.

For perennials, choose yarrow, hollyhock, pearly everlasting, rock cress, butterfly weed, coneflower, black-eyed Susan, daylily, phlox, lupine, bee balm or sedum. They'll start filling in and blooming the second year.

Then add evergreens and deciduous trees and shrubs like dogwood, viburnum, shrub rose, hawthorn and maple.

QUALITY BRAND
Country Kitchen
SUGAR
Best crystal sugar

Q: Do you have any tips for growing impatiens? I plant them in containers, fertilize and water them, but they still die.

A: First, be sure you're buying healthy plants. Always start with clean pots and fresh potting mix to eliminate the risk of diseases carrying over from one growing season to the next. Make sure to check the label on the potting mix before fertilizing, because some include a slow-release fertilizer. Buy those that don't, and add your own slow-release fertilizer at planting time. This often provides plants with all the nutrients they need for the season. If needed, add a midseason nutrient boost. Check on the containers daily, twice in hot weather, and water thoroughly when needed until the excess runs out the bottom. It's best to grow impatiens in a shady spot in a container with drainage holes, and to keep the soil slightly moist.

Q: My trumpet vine has only had one bloom in several years. What's wrong?

A: It can be tough, but trumpet vines require patience. First and foremost, they need to reach maturity before they start blooming. This can take several years after planting. It's important to avoid high-nitrogen fertilizers, because they promote leaf and stem growth while also preventing flowering. Trumpet vines develop an extensive root system that allows them to absorb nutrients from surrounding plant beds and nearby lawns. This means you need to be careful when fertilizing these areas. Use a low-nitrogen, slow-release fertilizer to increase your chance of having a beautiful, blooming vine.

Q: I'm having a hard time growing hummingbird vine. Any advice?

A: Several plants go by the name hummingbird vine. The large orange and yellow flowered trumpet vine *(Campsis radicans)* attaches to structures with its aerial roots.

The bright-orange, coral-red or scarlet blooming honeysuckle vine *(Lonicera* spp.) also attracts hummingbirds. It attaches itself to structures by twining around the support.

Once you know which variety you have, make sure you give it the support it needs. A brick wall is a good choice for trumpet vine, while a trellis or arbor is more suitable for the honeysuckle.

You may need to provide a bit of training and guidance in the beginning. Secure branches to the structure with twine or staking tape. Once the vine makes contact, it should continue to grow and cling to the structure on its own. Proper growing conditions and care should get your vine off and growing. Trumpet vine prefers full sun and well-draining soil. Avoid types of fertilization that encourage lots of leaves and no flowers. Honeysuckle vines, on the other hand, like full sun to part shade.

Q: Sometimes hummingbirds fly into blue spruce trees. What are they after?

A: Besides nectar, hummingbirds also eat—and feed their babies—small insects, which they gather from flowers, shrubs and trees. In the case of the blue spruce, not only are they finding insects there, but the sap the tree produces is a nourishing food for them. Often, yellow-bellied sapsuckers will drill holes in spruce trunks to release pools of sap. Hummingbirds feast on this treat, too.

Q: Are there plants that will survive sunny, dry conditions but attract birds and butterflies?

A: Look for native plants that tolerate your climate and attract birds and butterflies. Black-eyed Susan, bluebonnets, Indian blanket, Indian paintbrush, golden tickseed, mealycup sage, Mexican hat, prairie verbena, Texas lantana and Yaupon holly are just a few.

▲ Q: Hummingbirds love bee balm, but mine is not blooming. Why?

A: A lack of nutrients, phosphorous in particular, can cause poor flowering or none at all. Container planted bee balm especially, is usually grown in soilless mixes that don't retain nutrients and are watered daily, fertilizing regularly is crucial. Use a slow-release fertilizer at the start of the season, with a midseason application if needed. Or try using a flowering-plant fertilizer regularly. Follow label directions and stop fertilizing midseason to reduce the risk of winter damage.

◄ Q: Why do only female ruby-throated hummingbirds show up at feeders?

A: Male and female ruby-throats don't ever stay together as pairs. The male has a small territory where he courts any passing female and chases away other males. The female has her own home range, where she raises her young. If a female ruby-throat has her nest nearby, she may come to your feeder regularly; if the neighborhood male's center of activity is farther away, he may be getting his food elsewhere. So in early summer, it's partly a matter of luck.

Q: When should I start and stop feeding hummingbirds?

A: Early May is a good time to hang out your hummingbird feeders—except in the South, where migratory hummers begin tapping sugar-water feeders in early April. And don't hurry to take them down in fall. It's a myth that if you keep your feeders up, the hummingbirds won't migrate. When you leave your feeders in place through migration season, you'll catch any late travelers as they fly through your area.

Q: I have feeders but no hummingbirds. How can I attract them?

A: A surefire way to attract hummingbirds is to plant red flowers. Almost any red bloom—geraniums, impatiens, petunias, bee balm, honeysuckle, fuchsia—will entice them to visit a garden. Once you get their attention with the flowers, you can install feeders among the blooms and get them hooked on sugar water. Then you'll be able to move the feeders wherever you want them.

◄ Q: What is this little blue butterfly?

A: You've discovered the common checkered skipper, a butterfly that has two broods—one in spring and another in late summer and early fall. The butterfly's blue appearance comes from long, bluish hairs on the inner part of the wings. This species prefers fields and pastures with low-growing mallows, where it feeds.

The caterpillars of this butterfly make leaf nests by rolling or attaching a group of leaves together with silk near the top of mallow plants. The nests are fairly easy to find. If you carefully look inside, you will see the greenish caterpillar, with a dark head and covered with short, whitish hairs. The caterpillars will winter fully grown in these leaf shelters.

▼ Q: Butterflies love this flower. What is it?

A: It is a pinxterbloom azalea (*Rhododendron periclymenoides*). This low-growing azalea produces runners and lots of branches. It typically grows anywhere from 2 to 10 feet tall, and the fragrant flowers appear in spring. Tolerant of sandy, dry and rocky soils, this azalea is hardy in Zones 4 to 8.

Q: What can gardeners do to help the declining honeybee population get back on track?

A: You can help by stopping or minimizing your use of pesticides. To control garden pests, use eco-friendly methods like trapping, barriers and natural products, such as insecticidal soaps that are not harmful to bees.

Then plant a diverse garden filled with flowers suited to your climate that will provide nectar and pollen for the bees. Consider native plants whenever appropriate. A few honeybee favorites are sunflowers, goldenrod, coneflower, bee balm, grape hyacinths and ajuga. And don't forget about trees and shrubs such as apples, cherries, plums, redbud, abelia, blueberries, blackberries and hollies, and vegetables like pumpkin, eggplant and peas.

Q: Do butterfly houses attract butterflies?

A: Butterfly houses are more of a garden decoration than a way to attract butterflies to your yard.

Although a few butterfly species seek shelter for winter hibernation or a shady roost during the summer, most butterflies usually rest on vegetation or in trees.

However, if you put your houses in a protected area near woodlands, you could attract a mourning cloak or question mark. And in areas where Milbert's tortoiseshells are found, a butterfly house might be effective, since these butterflies hibernate in large groups.

Be aware, however, that butterfly houses also make good homes for wasps and hornets.

▼ Q: Is this a hummingbird moth?

A: Yes, this is one of the hummingbird moths, also known as sphinx moths or hawk moths. You can find more than 100 species in this family in North America. Many of them take nectar by hovering in front of flowers, very much like a hummingbird. Some species are active only at night, but this one, the white-lined sphinx, will visit flowers in daylight, so it's regularly seen in gardens. Its caterpillars feed on the leaves of a wide variety of host plants.

Q: Is it possible to create mud puddles to attract butterflies?

A: Butterflies sit on the damp mud and suck water up through their long, tubelike "tongues" (the proboscis). They may be partly just thirsty for water, but they're also taking in chemicals, especially some natural salts. So if you're making an artificial puddle, it's best to use something that's close to natural soil, plus rainwater or other untreated water if possible.

Q: How can I start *Verbena bonariensis* from seed?

A: Many people struggle to grow this beauty from seed. Give the seeds a cold treatment in the refrigerator for two weeks prior to sprouting. Place the seeds in moistened compost in a plastic bag or just plant the seeds and place the whole container in the refrigerator. Then move to a 65-degree location for germination. Be patient, though; it can take 28 days or more for seeds to germinate. Grow seedlings in a bright location or under artificial lights with good air circulation.

BACKYARD TIP
Verbena is disease-resistant and a great container plant. What more could you ask for?

Verbena

CHAPTER NINE
Backyard Projects & Resources

A Bird for the Birds

This little birdhouse is simple, sweet and versatile! If you can find a box that matches the approximate size needed, then you'll be able to make this birdhouse almost before you can say "black-capped chickadee!"

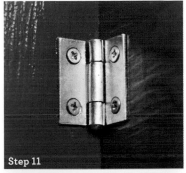
Step 11

Step 12

supplies

- 5-in.-square box (built, reclaimed or purchased)
- Lauan for "bird" shape
- Small finish nails
- Picture-hanging hardware or wire and 2 screws
- 1-in. butt hinge
- Screen door hook and eye
- Glue
- Exterior latex primer and paint
- Shellac or other outdoor varnish
- Bird template
- Jigsaw
- Screw gun or drill
- 1¼-in. to 1½-in. hole saw
- Clamps
- Hammer
- Fine-grit sandpaper

INSTRUCTIONS

NOTE: If you are building the box, follow the instructions from step 1. If you already have a box, begin with step 6.

STEP 1. Cut one 5x5-in. square, two 5x4¾-in. rectangles and two 4¾x4½-in. rectangles out of ¼-in. plywood, clear pine, shelf board, barn board or similar.

STEP 2. Glue one 5x4¾-in. rectangle to one 4¾x4½-in. rectangle. The 4¾-in. dimension is the height of both rectangles. Once joined, they will form an "L" with a short side, and a longer side but both the same height. Clamp until dry. Repeat with the other 2 rectangles.

STEP 3. Glue the two L-shaped side sections to the 5-in.-square box bottom. Make sure that the sections come together to form a perfect square. Clamp until dry.

STEP 4. Once dry, reinforce the joints with small finish nails or brads.

STEP 5. Sand box with fine-grit sandpaper in preparation for painting.

STEP 6. Print out the template (at left) and cut out the bird shape.

STEP 7. Trace bird onto lauan; cut out with the jigsaw.

STEP 8. Using a hole saw attached to a screw gun or drill, bore a 1¼-in. to 1½-in. hole in the lauan. This is the bird's entrance, so be sure to place it accordingly.

STEP 9. Sand the face and edges smooth in preparation for painting.

STEP 10. Prime and paint the outside of the box and bird shape, leaving the inside unpainted.

STEP 11. Hinge the bird cutout to the box using a simple 1-in. butt hinge or similar connector (see photo at top right).

STEP 12. Attach screw-eye with hook to the back of the bird and the other screw-eye to the side of the box so that they meet when the hook closes (see photo above).

STEP 13. Seal the outside of birdhouse with several coats of shellac.

STEP 14. Attach picture-hanging hardware to the back of the box.

Print out this template at 450% to accommodate a 5-in. box (dashed line).

Leafy Birdhouse

If you've never picked up a jar of Mod Podge, hurry to the nearest craft store. A combination glue and sealer, Mod Podge is easy to use and nontoxic. It's also the staple ingredient for this leafy birdhouse. There is no right or wrong when creating, so grab some leaves and garage leftovers, and have a little fun.

supplies

- Birdhouse
- Upcycled accessories
- Tree leaves (ligustrum, photinia, azaleas, crepe myrtle, laurel, holly, viburnum or a combination), flattened under a heavy book or tiles
- Mod Podge (Outdoor preferred)
- Artist's paintbrush
- Spray sealer (optional)
- Hot glue, screws or other fasteners

INSTRUCTIONS

STEP 1. Buy or build a birdhouse. Drill ventilation holes in the sides near the top, and drainage holes in the bottom. Add a predator guard, if possible, and a door for easy cleaning.

STEP 2. Choose accessories. Make a base out of a thrift-store find like an ashtray stand, a candlestick or lamp base, or old furniture legs—there are no rules, except the result should be stable. Lighting parts, door hardware and hinges, knobs and handles make great adornments.

STEP 3. Attach the base and adornments, using hot glue, screws or other fasteners, as needed.

STEP 4. Attach leaves: Using the artist's brush, paint the backside of a leaf with a thin layer of Mod Podge, press the leaf flat against the house, and then coat the topside of the leaf thinly with Mod Podge. Keep attaching leaves, one at a time, back and front, until the birdhouse is covered. Mod Podge dries quickly. Apply multiple layers, allowing each coat to dry completely before applying the next one. Several thin layers are more effective and attractive than one or two thick coats.

STEP 5. If you have used the indoor version of Mod Podge, add several thin coats of spray sealer to protect the leaves from the elements, allowing each coat to dry thoroughly before applying the next. (Omit this step if you have used Outdoor Mod Podge.)

DIY BEE ACCESSORY
Stir up some buzz with this handsome bee.

1 Cut a 2-in. piece of spindle from a broken chair or use a dowel or other cylindrical piece of wood. Sand it to round it out, paint it yellow and drill 8 holes—1 at the head of the body, 1 at the tail, 2 on the topside for wings and 4 on the underside for legs.

2 At the head end, insert a short length of wire for one antenna. Insert another short length at the tail for the stinger. Take a long length of wire, twist it around the stinger, around the body, and then coil it several times around the antenna to form the head. Bend the end of the same piece to form the second antenna, trimming excess. Insert a short length of wire in each of the 4 bottom holes for the legs.

3 Form 2 lengths of wire into wings, leaving enough at the ends to insert in the top holes. Spray with varnish or shellac. Attach to the birdhouse with weather-resistant adhesive or by bending the legs slightly to grip the sides of the house.

Nest Box in an Instant

Some birds are not picky—a cute nesting platform made from recycled materials is sometimes all it takes to lure in common nesters, like American robins, wrens and mourning doves. Look for a small galvanized bucket that might need a new life. An item like this is perfect—not too big or too small, with sweet angled sides and a wire handle.

supplies

- Old bucket
- Hammer and nails
- Screwdriver and wood screw
- Wire
- Needle-nose pliers
- Spray paint

INSTRUCTIONS

STEP 1. Paint the bucket. Painting is often the easiest way to transform the ordinary into something snazzy. Pumpkin-orange spray paint was used for the outside of this bucket and metallic silver for the inside. If your bucket is in newer condition, you could leave the inside unpainted.

STEP 2. Plan the attachment. If you're attaching the bucket directly onto a porch column, just drill a hole in the center of the bucket. But if you think you might attach your nesting box differently, make sure it's ready to hang before accessorizing it with any delicate or decorative objects.

STEP 3. Adorn the bucket. The shape of this bucket looks kind of like a head, so we added something that resembled a hat made of wire. It's a good option for adorning because wire bends, and birds (unlike bigger critters) have no problem perching on it. The bucket's wire handles help with any attachments.

STEP 4. Find a site and hang. When choosing a location, keep in mind that Carolina wrens and robins are the most likely birds to take up residence in a nest box. Carolina wren nests are frequently found near homes, usually 3 to 6 feet off the ground, and in odd places. Robins' nests tend to be in the lower halves of trees, as well as in gutters or eaves, and on outdoor light fixtures and other structures.

7 MORE GREAT SHELTER IDEAS

BASKETS. Easter baskets, market reed baskets or small thrift store baskets are easily adorned with greens and other small decorations.

OLD MAILBOXES. A wall-mounted mailbox can be attached to a tree, under eaves or on a column, while a post-mounted model can be perched on a fence post or tree stump.

CARDBOARD BOXES. The right-sized cardboard box can be roofed with rubber or metal, sealed on the exterior with shellac or varnish, then decorated.

KITCHENWARE. Whether it's a copper garlic holder or stainless steel pasta pot, don't overlook common household items. A cupboard or closet can be a gold mine of ideas!

GARDEN POTS. A terra-cotta pot already has a hole in the bottom. Add a screw and a washer, and it's ready for mounting. All you have to do is embellish it.

OLD PORCH LIGHTS. We've all seen the nests in our porch lights. If you replace an old one, don't throw it away. Often, just a few adjustments make it display-worthy and bird-friendly.

PAINT BUCKETS. The 1 gallon metal kind is a nice size. Just make sure to hang it in a shady spot, so it won't get too hot.

Feeder from a Frame

If you have a picture frame lying around—maybe the glass broke or you found it at a thrift store—turn it into a delightful bird feeder.

supplies

- Old picture frame
- 4 screw eyes
- Chain or wire for hanging
- Shower curtain hanger or something similar for gathering the chain
- Window screen
- Paint
- Staple gun and staples
- Wire cutters (if using stiff chain)
- Snips or scissors for cutting screen
- Hammer and finish nail or drill bit for pilot holes

INSTRUCTIONS

STEP 1. Paint your picture frame, if desired.

STEP 2. Cut your screen to fit your picture frame opening and staple it to the back. (The staples went through to the frame's front, so you might use caulk as if it was cake icing to cover them up and make a fake filigree!)

STEP 3. Using either a hammer and finish nail or drill bit, make pilot holes in the four corners of the finished side of the frame for your screw eyes. Twist in the screw eyes.

STEP 4. Cut four equal lengths of chain or wire and attach one to each screw eye. Gather at the top and run your shower curtain hanger through the ends of the chain. Hang from the nearest branch!

5-Minute Feeder

Orioles will flock to this feeder! Fill it with grape jelly or homemade sugar water in early spring and wait for the orioles to arrive.

supplies

- 3 ft. 10-gauge copper wire
- 12 in. 18-gauge copper wire
- Double shot glass (3 oz.)
- Wire strippers or cutters
- Needle-nose pliers
- Pen
- Glass beads

INSTRUCTIONS

STEP 1. Using the needle-nose pliers, make a small hook at one end of the 10-gauge wire. This will be the feeder's hanger.

STEP 2. Starting at the hanger end, gently bend the wire into an arch. You can use a round object to help with this or you can bend it freehand.

STEP 3. Approximately 12 in. from the hanger end, bend the wire at about a 45-degree angle. Place the shot glass on top of the wire and bend the wire around the bottom.

STEP 4. Cup the wire and glass in one hand while wrapping most of the remaining wire tightly around the glass.

STEP 5. At this point, you should have about 6 to 8 in. of wire remaining. Curve it into a "C" shape in front of the glass to make a perch.

STEP 6. To help the feeder hang better, gently twist the main part of the hanger a quarter turn to the right or left.

STEP 7. Next, to decorate, take the 18-gauge copper wire and start wrapping it around the 10-gauge wire near the top of the hanger.

STEP 8. Wrap the last few inches of wire around a pen to make a curlicue.

STEP 9. Attach beads in alternating sizes. To secure the beads, curl the end of the wire with needle-nose pliers.

Budget Bird Feeder

This discarded tomato cage is a wonderful feeder for the birds!
Add a few tin flowers, an arching plant and a colorful dish for birdseed,
and you'll soon have happy birds and a bona fide work of art.

supplies

- Tomato cage
- Plastic pot with plants
- Plastic bowl or tray
- Flat, thin metal
- Tin snips
- Spray paint
- Hammer and nail
- Needle-nose pliers
- Wire

FEEDER INSTRUCTIONS

STEP 1. If you already have a location in mind, install your tomato cage to start. You can either insert the tines into the earth as you would normally (the deeper and more even, the better), or bend the tines outward to form "feet."

STEP 2. Measure the circumference of the tomato cage ring that you want to use for holding up your plant. Arrange plants in a plastic pot with a top circumference slightly larger than the ring on the cage. Ease it into place.

STEP 3. Measure the very top ring of the tomato cage for a plastic bowl or tray to rest there, and then scout around for a colorful receptacle that fits your dimensions. Your kitchen, yard sales and thrift stores are great options.

STEP 4. Make the flowers. (See flower assembly steps.) Twist the wire stems around the vertical tines of the cage.

STEP 5. Last but not least, drop the bowl or tray into the top ring of the cage, and add birdseed.

FLOWER INSTRUCTIONS

STEP 1. Draw a simple flower shape on your choice of metal and cut 2 or more with tin snips or similar metal-cutting tool.

STEP 2. Cut out one small center circle for each two flowers you cut.

STEP 3. Spray-paint flowers and circles in the colors of your choice.

STEP 4. Nestle two of the flowers together and place one circle on top in the center. Using a nail and a hammer, punch a hole in the center of the flower cluster with a whack of the hammer on the nail. Repeat for all flowers.

STEP 5. Take about 12 in. of wire that is stiff enough to hold the flowers upright but flexible enough to bend easily. Using needle-nose pliers, twist a loop in the wire about 2 in. from one end. This will support the flowers so they don't fall straight down the wire.

STEP 6. Thread the flower cluster onto the short end of the wire to rest on the loop you made, and twist the wire above the flower into a spiral using needle-nose pliers. This will sandwich the flowers between loops so they are secure. Repeat for the rest of the flowers, and you're ready to attach them to the tomato cage.

CHOOSING A BOTTLE

Glass bottles larger than 375 ml are heavy and more prone to leakage. Thus, they are not recommended for this project. Above all, the bottle must provide a tight fit for the stopper portion of the feeding tube you buy.

Anything less than an airtight fit will allow the nectar to drip from the feeding tube. Many soda and water bottles are a good fit for a commercial tube feeder assembly. Be sure to test the seal before you complete your design and add sugar water.

A Bottle for Hummingbirds

Forget buying expensive, decorative sugar-water feeders. Now you can make your own for just a few bucks by using a recycled bottle. You'll be amazed at how fun and easy it is to make this one-of-a-kind feeder using a glass bottle. And with the copper accents, it's a decorative addition to your backyard, too.

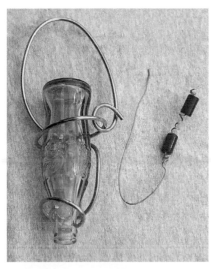

supplies

- Glass bottle
- 5 ft. of 4-gauge untreated copper wire
- 3 to 5 ft. of 12-gauge untreated copper wire
- Hummingbird feeding tube
- Beads or other decorations
- D-ring or carabiner
- Screw eye
- File
- Needle-nose pliers
- Wire cutter

INSTRUCTIONS

STEP 1. File the ends of the copper wires so there are no sharp edges.

STEP 2. Take the 4-gauge wire and bend it at one of the ends to form a small circle. This should fit loosely over the opening of the bottle.

STEP 3. Insert the bottle in the circle, and make one more loop around the neck to hold it securely.

STEP 4. With the neck of the bottle securely in the two loops, wind the rest of the wire around the bottle. (You have a little freedom to create your own design.) The wire should be loose enough to easily remove the bottle for refilling the sugar water, but tight enough to hold the feeder securely.

STEP 5. Bend the last 18 inches or so of wire upward to make a hanging hook and then fashion a loop at the very end to secure it, as shown.

STEP 6. Next, decorate your feeder using the 12 gauge copper wire.

STEP 7. Use needle-nose pliers and wire cutters to shape the wire as needed. Here's a design tip: To create the look of curling vines, wrap the wire around a pencil first and then attach it in pieces.

STEP 8. Use colorful beads or other adornments to complete your design. Remember, hummingbirds love red, so it's a great accent color.

STEP 9. Remove the bottle and fill with sugar water. Gently twist the stopper of the store-bought feeding tube into place at the opening of the bottle. It should fit snugly to avoid leaking.

STEP 10. After you fill it with sugar water, place the bottle back into the copper holder. You might have to shake the bottle a little to dislodge any air bubbles. If it leaks, remove the feeding tube and try repositioning the stopper to get a more snug fit.

STEP 11. Ready to put your feeder to work? Make sure it hangs securely by hooking the feeder onto a snap ring or carabiner. Put the ring through a screw eye and hang the entire feeder in the desired location. Then, sit back, relax and watch for hummingbirds. Change the sugar water every few days.

NOTE: We placed this fountain in dappled sun to get a good photo, but remember, full sun is best long-term.

Bringing Solar to the Garden

This is a really simple project. The most vital step is picking a sunny location for your pots before you start. This is important for two reasons. First, the fountain will work only when the sun is shining directly on the solar panels. Second, once the fountain is assembled, it'll probably be too heavy to move! Pick up some pretty pots and a solar fountain pump this year—you'll have a new water feature and planter for your yard in no time.

supplies

- 2 pots of different sizes
- Platform to go in larger pot
- Soil
- Plants
- Solar-powered fountain unit (see Step 6)

INSTRUCTIONS

STEP 1. This project starts at the garden center where you choose your containers. In the picture, you'll see that the fountain features a smaller pot nestled in a larger one. (The third pot visible behind the large one is not necessary.) While you're at the store, test out different pots to see how they look together. You'll want to make sure the proportions are right before you get them home.

STEP 2. If your containers have drainage holes, you'll need to plug the holes of the smaller one, which will hold water for the fountain. We used cork to plug the hole and then covered it with heavy-duty plastic using hot glue. You don't have to use cork, but choose a material that won't deteriorate. Make sure all the edges of the plastic are glued down and everything is dry. To check for leaks, pour a pitcher of water into the pot. And if your large pot doesn't have drainage holes, drill a few in the bottom so your soil won't be soggy.

STEP 3. Put the platform in the larger pot. The one pictured here uses a wooden platform fitted about halfway down into the container. If you're using round pots, you could also use an Ups-A-Daisy planter insert, which you can check out at *ups-a-daisy.com*.

STEP 4. Place the smaller pot in the larger one, setting it firmly on the platform insert. Make sure it's level and secure. Then fill the space between the pots with potting soil.

STEP 5. Slowly add water to the top pot, making sure the pot stays level and safely seated in the soil. When the small pot is full, plant your flowers or greenery in the large pot and pack the soil tightly around the small pot to keep it secure. Water the plants until the water seeps out the drainage hole of the bottom pot, adding soil as necessary.

STEP 6. Finally, unpack and assemble the solar fountain and place it in the small pot. We used a self-contained unit where the solar panels float on the water. Other models have solar panels that are connected to the pump with wires, with the panel generally stuck into the ground some distance away. The latter, which are designed mostly for ponds, won't work as well for this project.

STEP 7. As the water evaporates, add more. And don't forget to water your plants, too!

Mosaic Birdbath

Ready to get crafty? Attract birds in style with this simple do-it-yourself birdbath. It might look difficult and expensive, but it's really quite easy and cheap to make.

supplies

- 12-in. terra-cotta saucer
- Terra-cotta sealer
- Approximately 300 ⅜-in. glass tiles of your choice
- Water-resistant tile adhesive
- Sanded grout in your choice of color
- Outdoor penetrating grout sealer
- Foam paintbrush
- Paper towels
- Tile cutters
- Plastic knife
- Rubber gloves
- Several soft cloths
- Sponge
- Safety glasses
- Dust mask

INSTRUCTIONS

STEP 1. Rinse terra-cotta saucer to remove dust and debris. Allow to dry overnight before sealing.

STEP 2. Seal all saucer surfaces with a terra-cotta sealer. Allow to dry at least two hours before gluing on mosaic pieces.

STEP 3. Using the plastic knife, apply a thin layer of adhesive to the back of each tile. Press the tile, adhesive side down, to the saucer. (It is easiest to start gluing from the outside of the pattern and then work your way in.)

STEP 4. Allow no more than ¼ in. between the pieces and try to keep the distance the same between all the pieces. This will add strength to your birdbath and will be more pleasing to the eye.

STEP 5. If you'd like to create a specific pattern or design, it's good to have a pair of tile cutters handy. For example, you could cut some tiles diagonally.

STEP 6. Once all the tiles are in place, allow the adhesive to dry for at least 24 hours before grouting.

STEP 7. Cover your work surface and put on a dust mask before you begin mixing the grout, as the dust from dry grout can harm your lungs. Mix the sanded grout according to package directions. You can remove the dust mask once the grout has been mixed and is no longer powdery. Your grout should be the consistency of peanut butter when completely mixed. If it's too wet, the grout will be weaker and harder to clean up.

STEP 8. Allow grout to sit five to 10 minutes before applying it to the saucer. If you buy premixed grout, make sure it is sanded grout for outdoor use.

STEP 9. Wearing rubber gloves, apply grout by hand or with a plastic putty knife. Press grout between all the pieces and smooth with your fingers. When applying grout to the rim of the saucer, make sure the edge of each tile is completely covered and is smooth to the touch. Allow the grout to sit for 20 to 60 minutes or until it begins to dry. Then wipe off any excess grout with a dry cloth.

STEP 10. Allow the grout to sit for an additional 30 to 60 minutes. Then fill a bucket with warm water, wet your sponge, wring it out well and use it to wipe off any film.

STEP 11. You may have to wipe your piece several times over the course of an hour or two. Rinse and wring the sponge often for best results. If a film keeps forming on the piece, either your sponge is too wet or dirty or you need to let the grout dry a little longer before wiping it down.

STEP 12. After several hours, buff the tiles with a clean soft cloth to remove the last of the film.

STEP 13. Allow the grout to dry at least 24 hours before sealing with an outdoor penetrating sealer. Follow manufacturer's instructions. Usually you will need to apply the sealer with a foam paintbrush. Allow the sealer to dry for five to 10 minutes, then wipe off the excess with a paper towel.

STEP 14. Allow birdbath to dry for two hours, then apply another coat of sealer.

STEP 15. Leave the outside unpainted or apply an outdoor acrylic paint.

Create a base by gluing two 12-in. terra-cotta pots together.

BIRDBATH MAINTENANCE

You can leave your birdbath out year-round, but if it's painted or stained, you may want to bring it inside during winter. Clean it just as you would any other birdbath, using a sponge or small brush once a week.

Break the Mold

Capture the natural beauty of a leaf in this elegant birdbath! You don't have to pay a lot for a one-of-a-kind birdbath. At planting time, look for plants with large leaves to add to your garden. Then turn one of those big beauties into a birdbath. This project makes a serene resting place for butterflies, too.

supplies

- Large leaf
- ½ to 1 bag of play sand
- 3 to 4 cups of contractor's sand
- 1 to 2 cups Portland cement
- Concrete fortifier

INSTRUCTIONS

STEP 1. Choose a leaf at least 10 in. long and 7 in. wide. (We used a hosta leaf here, but rhubarb, burdock, gunnera, castor bean, caladium and elephant-ear leaves also work well.) Cut the stem off.

STEP 2. Spread out a plastic sheet or a large plastic bag to protect your work surface. Pour the play sand onto the plastic and make a pile. Wet the sand slightly so that it sticks together, the way you would for a sandcastle.

STEP 3. Shape the pile to approximate the size and shape of your leaf, but keep in mind that birds do not like baths that are more than a couple of inches deep. Once the sand pile is to your liking, cover it with a piece of plastic or a plastic bag. Place the leaf vein-side up on top of the plastic, centering it.

STEP 4. In a plastic bowl, mix three parts contractor's sand to one part Portland cement. Mix ¼ cup of water and ¼ cup of concrete fortifier, and add slowly to the sand until it reaches the consistency of a thick brownie batter. The easiest way to do this is to squish it with your hands wearing rubber gloves. Mix more water and fortifier to add to the sand if needed.

STEP 5. Rinse your gloves or hands. Pick up a handful of the sand mixture, plop it on the center of the leaf and spread to the edges. This gives you a solid surface that picks up the leaf's veining while removing air bubbles.

STEP 6. Now slowly start building up the thickness of the casting. For strength, keep it between ½ and 1 in. thick. Be careful to keep the edges smooth to get a good contour. Once you have it at a good thickness, build up the center to make a pedestal.

STEP 7. Cover the mixture loosely with plastic. If it's a hot day, you might want to mist the casting from time to time to keep it from drying out too fast and cracking. Let your project dry slowly for about 24 hours, then peel off the leaf. If the casting feels brittle, let it sit for another day.

STEP 8. After the casting has dried for a good week, you can paint or seal it. (We painted this one green.) Or just leave it as is!

Step 3

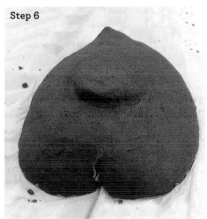
Step 6

Step 8

Do you know your state butterfly?

OREGON
Oregon Swallowtail

MONTANA
Mourning Cloak

IDAHO
Monarch

MINNESOT
Monarc

COLORADO
Colorado Hairstreak

CALIFORNIA
California Dogface

ARIZONA
Two-Tailed Swallowtail

NEW MEXICO
Sandia Hairstreak

OKLAHOMA
Black Swallowtail

TEXAS
Monarch

HAWAII
Pulelehua

LOVE BUTTERFLIES?

Our friends at Gardens With Wings provided this list for us. For helpful tips on attracting butterflies near you, check out *gardenswithwings.com*.

Take a minute to learn about these honored representatives.

Many people know their state bird and flower, but their state butterfly? Who knew that was even a thing? Technically, in most cases, they're state insects, but take a look at this wide butterfly representation.

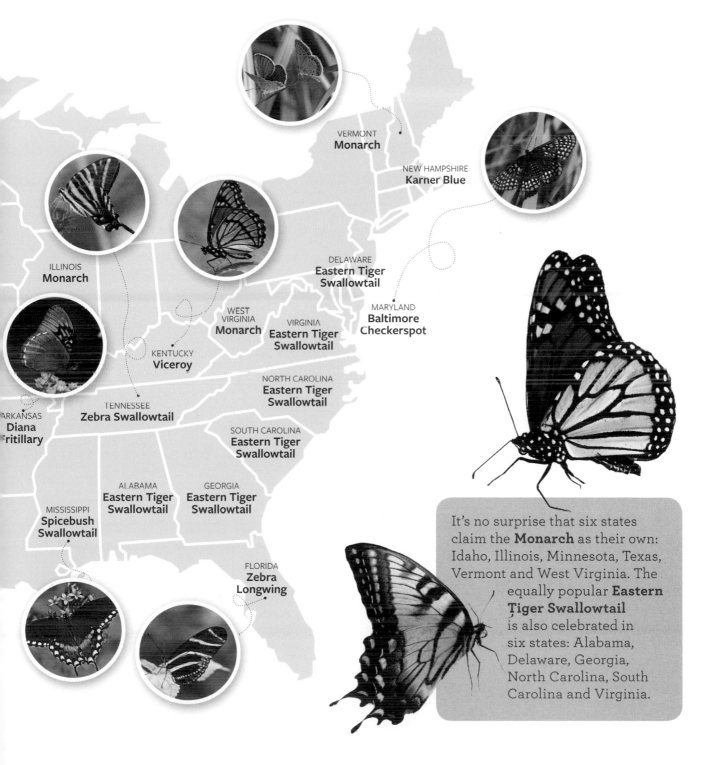

VERMONT
Monarch

NEW HAMPSHIRE
Karner Blue

ILLINOIS
Monarch

DELAWARE
Eastern Tiger Swallowtail

WEST VIRGINIA
Monarch

VIRGINIA
Eastern Tiger Swallowtail

MARYLAND
Baltimore Checkerspot

KENTUCKY
Viceroy

NORTH CAROLINA
Eastern Tiger Swallowtail

ARKANSAS
Diana Fritillary

TENNESSEE
Zebra Swallowtail

SOUTH CAROLINA
Eastern Tiger Swallowtail

ALABAMA
Eastern Tiger Swallowtail

GEORGIA
Eastern Tiger Swallowtail

MISSISSIPPI
Spicebush Swallowtail

FLORIDA
Zebra Longwing

It's no surprise that six states claim the **Monarch** as their own: Idaho, Illinois, Minnesota, Texas, Vermont and West Virginia. The equally popular **Eastern Tiger Swallowtail** is also celebrated in six states: Alabama, Delaware, Georgia, North Carolina, South Carolina and Virginia.

Native Plants Chart

Attract more birds and butterflies by including native plants in your landscape.

	COMMON NAME	SCIENTIFIC NAME	HARDINESS ZONES	FLOWER COLOR	HEIGHT	BLOOM TIME	SOIL MOISTURE
DRY SOILS AND DRY CLIMATES (15"–25" ANNUAL PRECIPITATION)	**Leadplant**	*Amorpha canescens*	3-8	Purple	2'–3'	June-July	D, M
	Butterfly weed	*Asclepias tuberosa*	3-10	Orange	2'–3'	June-Aug.	D, M
	Smooth aster	*Aster laevis*	4-8	Blue	2'–4'	Aug.-Oct.	D, M
	Cream false indigo	*Baptisia bracteata*	4-9	Cream	1'–2'	May-June	D, M
	Purple prairie clover	*Dalea purpurea*	3-8	Purple	1'–2'	July-Aug.	D, M
	Pale purple coneflower	*Echinacea pallida*	4-8	Purple	3'–5'	June-July	D, M
	Prairie smoke	*Geum triflorum*	3-6	Pink	6"	May-June	D, M
	Dotted blazing star	*Liatris punctata*	3-9	Purple/Pink	1'–2'	Aug.-Oct.	D, M
	Wild lupine	*Lupinus perennis*	3-8	Blue	1'–2'	May-June	D
	Large-flowered beardtongue	*Penstemon grandiflorus*	3-7	Lavender	2'–4'	May-June	D
	Showy goldenrod	*Solidago speciosa*	3-8	Yellow	1'–3'	Aug.-Sept.	D, M
	Bird's-foot violet	*Viola pedata*	3-9	Blue	6"	Apr.-June	D
MEDIUM SOILS IN AVERAGE RAINFALL CLIMATES (25"–45" ANNUAL PRECIPITATION)	**Nodding pink onion**	*Allium cernuum*	3-8	White/Pink	1'–2'	July-Aug.	M, Mo
	New England aster	*Aster novae-angliae*	3-7	Blue/Purple	3'–6'	Aug.-Sept.	M, Mo
	Blue false indigo	*Baptisia australis*	3-10	Blue	3'–5'	June-July	M, Mo
	White false indigo	*Baptisia lactea*	4-9	White	3'–5'	June-July	M, Mo
	Shooting star	*Dodecatheon meadia*	4-8	White/Pink	1'–2'	May-June	M, Mo
	Purple coneflower	*Echinacea purpurea*	4-8	Purple	3'–4'	July-Sept.	M, Mo
	Rattlesnake master	*Eryngium yuccifolium*	4-9	White	3'–5'	June-Aug.	M
	Prairie blazing star	*Liatris pycnostachya*	3-9	Purple/Pink	3'–5'	July-Aug.	M, Mo
	Wild quinine	*Parthenium integrifolium*	4-8	White	3'–5'	June-Sept.	M, Mo
	Yellow coneflower	*Ratibida pinnata*	3-9	Yellow	3'–6'	July-Sept.	M, Mo
	Royal catchfly	*Silene regia*	4-9	Red	2'–4'	July-Aug.	M
	Stiff goldenrod	*Solidago rigida*	3-9	Yellow	3'–5'	Aug.-Sept.	M, Mo
MOIST SOILS AND MOIST CLIMATES (45"–60" ANNUAL PRECIPITATION)	**Wild hyacinth**	*Camassia scilloides*	4-8	White	1'–2'	May-June	M, Mo
	Tall Joe Pye weed	*Eupatorium fistulosum*	4-9	Purple/Pink	5'–8'	Aug.-Sept.	Mo, W
	Queen of the prairie	*Filipendula rubra*	3-6	Pink	4'–5'	June-July	M, Mo
	Bottle gentian	*Gentiana andrewsii*	3-6	Blue	1'–2'	Aug.-Oct.	Mo, W
	Rose mallow	*Hibiscus palustris*	4-9	Pink	3'–6'	July-Sept.	Mo, W
	Dense blazing star	*Liatris spicata*	4-10	Purple/Pink	3'–6'	Aug.-Sept.	Mo, W
	Cardinal flower	*Lobelia cardinalis*	3-9	Red	2'–5'	July-Sept.	Mo, W
	Marsh phlox	*Phlox glaberrima*	4-8	Red/Purple	2'–4'	June-July	M, Mo
	Sweet black-eyed Susan	*Rudbeckia subtomentosa*	3-9	Yellow	4'–6'	Aug.-Oct.	M, Mo
	Ohio goldenrod	*Solidago ohioensis*	4-5	Yellow	3'–4'	Aug.-Sept.	M, Mo
	Tall ironweed	*Vernonia altissima*	4-9	Red/Pink	5'–8'	Aug.-Sept.	Mo, W
	Culver's root	*Veronicastrum virginicum*	3-8	White	3'–6'	July-Aug.	M, Mo

SOIL MOISTURE KEY

D = Dry (Well-drained sandy and rocky soils), **M** = Medium (Normal garden soils such as loam, sandy loam and clay loam),
Mo = Moist (Soils that stay moist below the surface, but are not boggy; may dry out in late summer),
W = Wet (Soils that are continually moist through the growing season, subject to short periods of spring flooding)

GARDENING FOR BIRDS, BUTTERFLIES & BEES

Backyard Color Guide

Boost your butterflies, tempt more hummingbirds or bring
in the bees by planting more of their favorite colors.

WHITE OR PALE COLOR

ATTRACTS: Night-flying moths; bats, in some areas

FLOWERS: Moonflower, angel's trumpet (*Datura* or
Brugmansia), white or pale-hued petunias, evening primrose

RED OR ORANGE

ATTRACTS: Hummingbirds

FLOWERS: Scarlet honeysuckle, bee balm, columbines,
canna, gladiolus, lilies, salvias, trumpet vine, ocotillo, azaleas

YELLOW

ATTRACTS: Butterflies

FLOWERS: Sunflowers, black-eyed Susans, gaillardia,
marigolds, golden alyssum

BLUE TO BLUE-PURPLE

ATTRACTS: Bees

FLOWERS: Crocus, hyacinth, grape hyacinth, salvias,
agastache, blue spirea, campanulas

PURPLE

ATTRACTS: Butterflies

FLOWERS: Butterfly bush, coneflower, asters, verbenas,
Russian sage, petunias, lavender, candytuft, agastache,
azaleas, rhododendrons

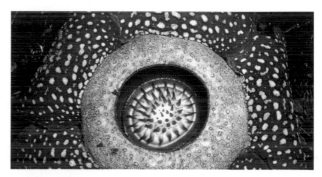

DULL RED OR RED-BROWN

ATTRACTS: Flies

FLOWERS: Wild ginger, Dutchman's pipe vine, trilliums,
pawpaw trees and some arums, including skunk cabbage;
another in this group is *Rafflesia arnoldii* (shown), the world's
largest flower, which boosts fly appeal, but has a fetid odor!

Birdhouse Guidelines

Discover which dwellings are best for your backyard birds.

SPECIES	DIMENSIONS	HOLE	PLACEMENT	COLOR	NOTES
Eastern bluebird	5x5x8″ h.	1½″ centered 6″ above floor	5-10′ high in the open; sunny area	light earth tones	likes open areas, especially facing a field
Tree swallow	5x5x6″ h.	1″ centered 4″ above floor	5-8′ high in the open; 50-100% sun	light earth tones or gray	within 2 miles of pond or lake
Purple martin	multiple apts. 6x6x6″ ea.	2⅛″ 2¼″ above floor	15-20′ high in the open	white	open yard without tall trees; near water
Tufted titmouse	4x4x8″ h.	1¼″	4-10′ high	light earth tones	prefers to live in or near woods
Chickadee	4x4x8″ h. or 5x5″ base	1⅛″ centered 6″ above floor	4-8′ high	light earth tones	small tree thicket
Nuthatch	4x4x10″ h.	1¼″ centered 7½″ above floor	12-25′ high on tree trunk	bark-covered or natural	prefers to live in or near woods
House wren	4x4x8″ h. or 4x6″ base	1″ centered 6″ above floor	5-10′ high on post or hung in tree	light earth tones or white	prefers lower branches of backyard trees
Northern flicker	7x7x18″ h.	2½″ centered 14″ above floor	8-20′ high	light earth tones	put 4″ sawdust inside for nesting
Downy woodpecker	4x4x10″ h.	1¼″ centered 7½″ above floor	12-25′ high on tree trunk	simulate natural cavity	prefers own excavation; provide sawdust
Red-headed woodpecker	6x6x15″ h.	2″ centered 6-8″ above floor	8-20′ high on post or tree trunk	simulate natural cavity	needs sawdust for nesting
Wood duck	10x10x24″ h.	4x3″ elliptical 20″ above floor	2-5′ high on post over water, or 12-40′ high on tree facing water	light earth tones or natural	needs 3-4″ of sawdust or shavings for nesting
American kestrel	10x10x24″ h.	4x3″ elliptical 20″ above floor	12-40′ high on post or tree trunk	light earth tones or natural	needs open approach on edge of woodlot or in isolated tree
Screech-owl	10x10x24″ h.	4x3″ elliptical 20″ above floor	2-5′ high on post over water, or 12-40′ high on tree	light earth tones or natural	prefers open woods or edge of woodlot

Note: With the exception of wrens and purple martins, birds do not tolerate swaying birdhouses. Birdhouses should be firmly anchored to a post, a tree or the side of a building.

Source: *Garden Birds of America* by George H. Harrison. Willow Creek Press, 1996.

Birds and Their Favorite Foods

	Nyjer (thistle) seed	Cracked corn	White proso millet	Black-oil sunflower seed	Hulled sunflower seed	Beef suet	Fruit	Sugar water/ nectar*
Rose-breasted grosbeak				•	•			
Black-headed grosbeak				•	•			
Evening grosbeak		•	•	•	•			
Northern cardinal		•	•	•	•		•	
Indigo bunting	•				•			
Eastern towhee	•	•	•	•	•			
Dark-eyed junco	•	•	•	•	•			
White-crowned sparrow	•	•	•	•	•			
White-throated sparrow	•	•	•	•	•			
American tree sparrow	•	•	•		•			
Chipping sparrow	•	•	•		•			
Song sparrow	•	•	•		•			
House sparrow	•	•	•	•				
House finch	•	•	•	•	•			
Purple finch	•	•	•	•	•			
American goldfinch	•	•	•	•	•			
Pine siskin	•	•	•		•			
Scarlet tanager							•	•
Western tanager							•	•
Baltimore oriole							•	•
Red-winged blackbird		•		•	•			
Eastern bluebird							•	
Wood thrush							•	
American robin							•	
Gray catbird							•	
Northern mockingbird							•	
Brown thrasher							•	
Ruby-throated hummingbird								•
Anna's hummingbird								•
Broad-tailed hummingbird								•
Tufted titmouse	•			•	•	•		
Black-capped chickadee	•			•	•	•		
White-breasted nuthatch				•	•	•		
Carolina wren						•		
Cedar waxwing							•	
Woodpecker				•	•	•	•	
Scrub jay		•		•	•	•	•	
Blue jay		•		•	•	•	•	
Mourning Dove	•	•	•		•			
Northern Bobwhite		•	•		•			
Ring-necked pheasant		•	•		•			
Canada goose		•						
Mallard		•						

* To make sugar water, mix 4 parts water with 1 part sugar. Boil, cool and serve. Store leftovers in the refrigerator for up to a week. Change feeder nectar every three to five days.

Source: *Garden Birds of America* by George H. Harrison. Willow Creek Press, 1996.

What's Your Zone?

Find out which plants will thrive in your area.

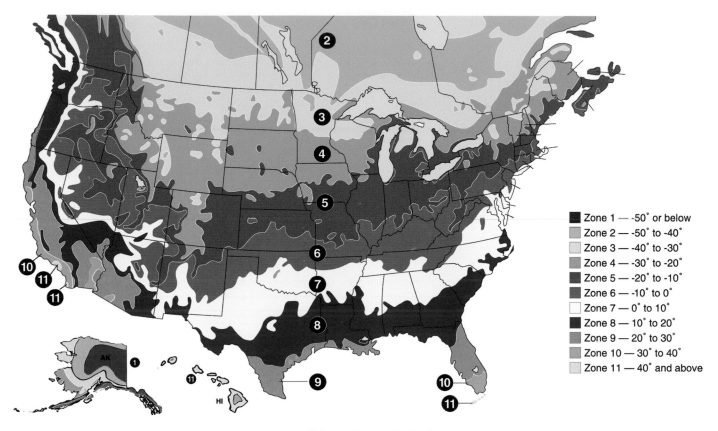

■	Zone 1 — -50° or below
■	Zone 2 — -50° to -40°
☐	Zone 3 — -40° to -30°
■	Zone 4 — -30° to -20°
■	Zone 5 — -20° to -10°
■	Zone 6 — -10° to 0°
☐	Zone 7 — 0° to 10°
■	Zone 8 — 10° to 20°
■	Zone 9 — 20° to 30°
■	Zone 10 — 30° to 40°
☐	Zone 11 — 40° and above

Map courtesy of the American Horticultural Society.
The zones featured in *Birds & Blooms Gardening for Birds, Butterflies & Bees*
should be treated as general guidelines when selecting plants for your garden.

Photo Credits

Nduche Onyeaso: p. 205

Richard Paul: p. 171, bottom

Paul Reeves Photography/Shutterstock.com: p. 20

Patricia Peck: p. 158, bottom

perennialresource.com: p. 60, bottom; p. 63, left; p. 64 bottom left; p. 64 bottom right; p. 66, top; p. 66, bottom; p. 67, bottom; p. 68; p. 69, top; p. 69, left; p. 73, top left; p. 73 bottom; p. 77, left; p. 80; p. 81, top; p. 82, bottom; p. 88, bottom; p. 91, bottom; p. 92, top; p. 93, bottom; p. 95, bottom; p. 102, left; p. 103, bottom; p. 106, left; p. 129, bottom; p. 147, bottom

Linda Persall: p. 196, bottom

Linda Petersen: p. 164, top; p. 167, bottom

Photo Resource Hawaii/Alamy: p. 242, pulelehua

picsbyst/Shutterstock.com: p. 25

Rod Planck/Dembinsky Photo: p. 195, bottom

Denis and Yulia Pogostins/Shutterstock.com: p. 37

provenwinners.com: p. 37, top; p. 39, bottom left; p. 40, bottom; p. 42; p. 44, top; p. 45, bottom; p. 47, bottom; p. 50, bottom; p. 56; p. 60, top; p. 65; p. 72; p. 75; p. 89, left; p. 100, bottom; p. 103, top; p. 105, left; p. 108, top; p. 112, top; p. 112, bottom right; p. 116, bottom; p. 117, bottom; p. 121, left; p. 145, top right; p. 146, left; p. 208, bottom right

Volker Rauch/Shutterstock.com: p. 144

Jeanne Raynes: p. 200, top

RDA-GID: p. 48; p. 51, bottom; p. 57, top; p. 59, bottom; p. 61, top; p. 63, bottom; p. 71, bottom; p. 74, bottom; p. 78 bottom; p. 79, bottom; p. 81, bottom; p. 82, top; p. 84; p. 85, top; p. 85, bottom; p. 92, bottom; p. 95, middle; p. 114, bottom; p. 122, top; p. 126, middle; p. 133, top; p. 147, top

RDA Milwaukee InHouse Stock CD: p. 45, top; p. 71, top; p. 74, top

Marie Read: p. 12; p. 13, bottom; p. 16; p. 209

REDA &CO srl/Alamy: p. 101

Mike Reese: p. 195, top; p. 203, top

Paul Rezendes: p. 193, bottom

Joyce Rick: p. 70; p. 161, bottom; p. 181, top; p. 182

ROBERT GEBBIE PHOTOGRAPHY/Shutterstock.com: p. 90, top

SUE ROBINSON/Shutterstock.com: p. 125, bottom

Kathy Rowland: p. 159, bottom

Rucron: p. 155, top

Rudyl: p. 153, left

Rachel Sachse: p. 34, top

Matteo Sani/Shutterstock.com: p. 34, top

Nick Saunders: p. 152, top; p. 165, bottom; p. 172, bottom; p. 177, bottom; p. 184, bottom; p. 185, left

Ellen L. Schmidt: p. 141, bottom

Ken R. Schneider: p. 242, Sandia hairstreak

Sandra Schumer: p. 163, top

sea-walker/Shutterstock.com: p. 94

Allen Blake Sheldon: p. 243, karner blue

Kathy Shelton: p. 198, bottom

SHSPhotography/Istock.com: p. 108, bottom

Dave Sim: p. 245, bottom left

Larry Simon/David Liebman: p. 201, top

Frederic B. Siskind: p. 2

Carolyn Smith: p. 183, middle

Katina Smith: p. 220

Randall C. Smith/Iseli Nursery: p. 124, left

snooker2009: p. 156, bottom

SOCK1979: p. 114, top

springstep: p. 159, top

Stepables.com: p. 57, bottom

sumamma2: p. 180, top

Raeann Sundholm: p. 198, top

SuperStock/Alamy: p. 242, Oregon swallowtail

LeeAnn Swonguer: p. 203, bottom

Gerald D. Tang: p. 243 Baltimore checkerspot

TERIELR: p. 123, bottom

TERRANOVANURSERIES.COM: p. 34, bottom; p. 62; p. 63, top; p. 69, bottom; p. 83, left; p. 87, bottom; p. 89, right; p. 90, bottom

Terry Wild Stock: p. 4; p. 17; p. 23

Mary Thall: p. 79, top

THDOLPHIN: p. 119, top

the sage: p. 158, top

Tucna: p. 154, top

Turner Photographics: p. 206; p. 242, two-tailed swallowtail

John & Gloria Tveten/KAC Productions: p. 192, bottom

Tom Uhlman/Alamy: p. 109, top

Tom Uhlman/the image finders: p. 163, bottom

USS Redbelly: p. 178, bottom

A & J Visage/Alamy: p. 245, bottom right

W. ATLEE BURPEE & CO: p. 38; p. 41, bottom; p. 43; p. 47, top; p. 48, bottom

Walters Gardens Inc.: p. 58 top; p. 98, top left; p. 98, top right; p. 212, left

Jane Webb: p. 199, top

Hugh Welford/Alamy: p. 99

Dave Welling: p. 24; p. 243, spicebush swallowtail

Steve Wenzl: p. 188, top

Rick Wetherbee: p. 115

Kathy White: p. 195, middle

WILDLIFE GmbH/Alamy: p. 142, top

Sam Wilson: p. 161, top; p. 175, left

WoodyStock/Alamy: p. 138, top

Index

Buttonbush

House finch

GARDENING FOR BIRDS, BUTTERFLIES & BEES

Blue jay

Pentas

Sunflower

Birds&Blooms